The
RUSSIAN VERSION
of the
SECOND WORLD WAR

The
RUSSIAN VERSION
of the
SECOND WORLD WAR

The History of the War
as Taught to Soviet Schoolchildren

Edited by Graham Lyons

Translated by Marjorie Vanston

Facts On File
Publications
New York

The Russian Version of the Second World War

Copyright © Graham Lyons 1976

First published in the United Kingdom in 1976.

Published in the United States of America by Facts On File, Inc.
460 Park Avenue South, New York, N.Y. 10016

Library of Congress Cataloging in Publication Data

Main entry under title:

The Russian version of the Second World War.

   Includes bibliographical references and index.
   1. World War, 1939-1945.   2. World War, 1939-1945—Study and teaching—Soviet Union.   I. Lyons, Graham, 1936-
D743.R87   1983   940.53   82-24236
ISBN 0-87196-136-9

Printed in the United States of America

10   9   8   7   6   5   4   3   2   1

CONTENTS

A section of photographs follows p. *62*

ACKNOWLEDGEMENTS

Firstly I must acknowledge the great debt which I owe to Marjorie Vanston who not only translated all the main text but much other material, a study of which was essential to the construction of the book. I must also thank the Society of Cultural Relations with the USSR for the use of their library.

Since the books from which my own text has been assembled were published before 1973 when the USSR became a signatory to the International Copyright Convention, there is no copyright on the use of the original texts. Nevertheless I must express my gratitude to the original authors without whom this book would never have existed.

FOREWORD

BY PROFESSOR BRIAN HOLMES
Professor of Education
Department of Comparative Education/University of London Institute of Education

The ease with which this book can be read should not disguise the seriousness of the compiler's purpose which is to show how the Second World War and some of the events leading up to it are presented to young people in the Soviet Union in their schools. If, to Western scholars and indeed to the layman, the interpretation of events seems oversimplified it should be remembered that versions of the war offered to pupils in Britain and the USA are likely to be slanted in another direction. Historical accounts of traumatic events are bound to include nationalistic sentiments. One way to ameliorate the harm this creates is to present to impressionable youngsters more than one account of events which destroyed the world of their parents and transformed their own lives.

For British parents the campaigns in France, North Africa and Burma probably loom large in their memory of the Second World War. For Americans the war in the Pacific and the invasion of occupied France perhaps occupy major positions. For the generation in the USSR who lived through and survived the invasion of their country, the sieges of Leningrad and Stalingrad and the defence of Moscow, the war on the Eastern Front is naturally regarded as being most significant in the defeat of the Nazi Forces. Understandably, however scholarly historians present their cases, teachers and parents pass on the folk-lore of hardships suffered and final triumphs enjoyed. Attempts to build up international understanding which pay no heed to this kind of background have little chance of success.

Therefore I congratulate Mr Lyons on compiling a lucid flowing account of the Second World War as seen through the eyes of Soviet authors. Regardless of whether or not readers agree with the interpretation offered, they should find the story fascinating and one which merits serious reflection. They might also like to know how memories of the war are kept alive in the USSR thirty years after the defeat of Germany. In 1975 the Cities of the Soviet Union displayed prominently banners celebrating the defeat of the Fascist invaders; books were published recalling the heroism of Soviet Citizens and doubtless many widows, widowers and orphans had reason to remember the immense losses suffered by their country in men and material. Mr Lyons' book admirably presents the background to feelings which remain very much alive today in the USSR.

BRIAN HOLMES

London, 1975

INTRODUCTION

Most of us have learned about the war from British and American writings. Particularly during the long Cold War period Western readers were given an unfavourable impression of Soviet policies and actions prior to and during the Second World War. British and American commentators presented these policies as being cynical, treacherous and immoral. Thus Russian cynicism was proved by the Hitler-Stalin non-aggression pact and Russian treachery by the Red Army invasion of Poland from the east while the Poles were desperately defending themselves against the German Army. In Western eyes the incorporation of the Baltic Republics into the Soviet Union was forced by Soviet threats and the Russian attack on Finland was further proof of the immorality of Russian methods. This behaviour seemed to follow exactly Hitler's way of dealing with smaller neighbouring states, while the massacre of Polish officers at Katyn perfectly imitated the methods of Stalin's new partner, though on a lesser scale.

In any Russian history, these events would naturally have to be written so as to reflect credit on the Soviet Union; yet with the given facts, this seems an impossible task. I say seems, because how can we be sure that our version is the 'right' one? Our opinions have been influenced by a predominantly anti-Russian slant (which sloped perilously steep in the Cold War), and there has been nothing for us to read from the Soviet side to set the record straight—or bend in the other direction! Equally, one would suspect that Russian historians would use some very sharp words when describing certain actions (or lack of action) by the Western Allies in the war.

The Cold War anti-Russian bias that permeated nearly all writing about the war must have affected our feelings about the Soviet Union. This bias was also apparent in Western school books. Thus millions of children have grown up with a distrust of the Soviet Union. And, judging by their history books, even more millions of Russian schoolchildren must have grown up with an even more pronounced distrust of the Western Allies.

If we want to know the feeling of a nation about great events in its history, the best possible sources are its school books. School history books are inevitably biased in their nation's favour in their selection of facts and in their comments. They are clearly and concisely written and give the flavour of a nation's attitude to its own history and to that of countries it has dealings with.

I have therefore prepared the main section of this book from two Russian schoolbooks: *Istoriya SSSR* by I. V. Bekhin, M. I. Belenkii and M. P. Kim published by Prosveshchenie Moscow, which deals in the main with the military aspects of the War, and *Noveishaya Istoriya* by P. M. Kuz'michev, G. R. Levin, V. A. Orlov, L. M. Predtechenskaya and V. K. Furaev, published also by Prosveshchenie, which covers the political side. These books are read by the pre-university class (equivalent to the British sixth form) throughout the Soviet Union.

The method of selecting and combining passages from the two books is as follows. Descriptions of particular events have been translated straight through using only one source. Thus the narrative under the heading 'The Attack on Poland' is the exact translation of a continuous Russian text under a similar heading. However, while the account of the battle of Stalingrad, for example, comes straight from the military book, the political implications of that battle have been taken from the second work, and together these extracts make up the chapter on Stalingrad. Sometimes lists of Soviet heroes and their exploits have been omitted, as have names of factories in the Urals, as being of slight interest to the non-specialist. I have also left out a sizeable chunk from the descriptions of campaigns in the year 1944. In this year the war had turned completely in favour of the Soviet Union and the factual descriptions of the battles are essentially the same as in any Western book. One of my objectives is to provide a logical and coherent narrative, and to do this, I have found it necessary in a few instances to change the order of the original material; and where there is needless repetition in the originals, I have trimmed passages. This book is not a précis of a longer work nor a selection from many different sources. The editing is purely in the interest of clarity. The spirit and the slant of the original text have been preserved.

I conceived this book for the general reader rather than for scholars, who could in any case refer to the sources quoted, and so I have deliberately avoided cluttering the text with footnotes giving the exact source reference for each passage. I would be happy to provide such information for anyone who cares to write to me c/o the publishers.

The editions of the school books used here have remained the same in all essentials since 1956, when Stalin, three years after his death, was denounced by Khruschev at the 20th Party Congress.

Before 1956 very little was published in the Soviet Union about the war and what little there was mentioned Stalin's name three times a page. Every engagement from the biggest to the smallest took place 'on the initiative of Stalin'. Stalin was credited with masterminding every single detail of a campaign. The rapid advances of the German armies in 1941 and 1942 were presented as preconceived by Stalin to draw the Wehrmacht deep into Russia and then to defeat the exhausted Germans by encirclement and crushing blows. 'All victories gained by the Soviet nation during the Great

Patriotic War* were due to the courage, daring, and genius of Stalin and no one else.'† It is interesting to see now how many times and in what role Stalin's name appears in this text.

As I have mentioned, many Soviet actions are considered extremely treacherous by Western opinion. This book gives an equal but opposite feeling of treachery by the Western Allies both before and during the war. A very strong feeling also arises from the book that the outcome of the war was decided exclusively on the Russian Front. Thus many events that we regard as heroic engagements are seen by the Russians as diversionary battles of no importance. For instance, the book points out that not one German division was removed from the Russian front during the whole of the North African Campaign.

At this point, I would like to make this one comment: it is unlikely that we in the West have a true idea of the scale and intensity of the fighting between Russia and Germany. And particularly the intensity. The war in the East was fought with a ferocity and a hatred not experienced by the British, French or Americans. A series such as 'Colditz' with Russian prisoners substituted for British would be laughable. Nazi Germany was a double-sided monster with its gentlemanly face turned westward and its ruthless inhuman skull pointed east.

The Great Patriotic War was the most cataclysmic event in the history of the Soviet Union. The horrors of that war and the terrifying consequences of a defeat have deeply affected every Soviet citizen who lived through it. This feeling must have been passed on to their children and when these children read what their history books say about

* The Russian name for their war with Germany.

† From *Special Report to the 20th Congress of the Communist Party of the Soviet Union* by N. S. Khruschev. This is obviously an ironic reference to Stalin's megalomania.

British, French and American diplomacy before the war and their frequent acts of treachery during the war, it is more than likely for them to remain, as adults, suspicious of all Western initiatives. Millions of Russians believe Britain and America acted in a strongly anti-Soviet way during the Soviet Union's most crucial years and we cannot fully understand the attitude of the Russians to us unless we know what they have learnt about us.

This version of the Second World War contradicts in many ways the established viewpoint in the West; there are also some surprising areas of convergence. The aim of this book is accurately and painlessly to satisfy the curiosity of those people in the West who want to find out exactly what is the official Soviet version of the Second World War and what their schoolchildren learn about it. Having read it, the reader can make up his own mind.

In the appendix, three of the most controversial issues—the Hitler-Stalin pact, the Finnish campaign and the Warsaw Uprising—are dealt with more fully than in the main text.

GRAHAM LYONS

1975

The
RUSSIAN VERSION
of the
SECOND WORLD WAR

CHAPTER I

★

International Relations on the Eve of the Second World War

✱

Prime Causes of the War

The Second World War was born of imperialism. The pursuit of the highest possible profits had often before driven the imperialists into wars of plunder. The greatest imperial powers aimed to seize territory that did not belong to them, to enslave the people of other countries and to dominate the world.

Relationships in the capitalist world prior to the First World War had been founded on the oppression of the weak by the strong, on dictatorship and arbitrary rule. The boundaries fixed by the Versailles Treaty after the First World War served the interests of the victorious powers only. This settlement carried within it the seed of a new world conflict.

In the 'thirties, this post-war structure started to crack. A conflict of interests began to develop between Germany, Italy and Japan on the one hand and England, France and the United States on the other.

The defeated countries wanted to take revenge and gain predominance over their competitors: they considered themselves deprived of their fair share. Germany, Italy and Japan were nurturing plans for the enslavement and physical extermination of many peoples. Hitlerite Germany and militarist Japan wanted to annihilate the Soviet Union, divide its territory between them, and transform Soviet citizens into slaves. The Fascist countries were intensely jealous of the colonies, sources of raw materials and markets for the sale of goods, which the other capitalist states possessed. They demanded for themselves 'a place in the sun'.

The imperialist group, consisting of England, France and the United States, opposed the Fascist coalition. These countries, having won the First World War, wished to preserve their victorious position and once again to weaken their rivals.

The world economic crisis greatly intensified the rivalry between the two capitalist blocs, but the basic contradiction in world affairs remained the conflict between socialism and capitalism.

Reactionary forces were preparing a war of all the imperialist states against the Soviet Union. However, the deep-rooted dissension which existed between the two imperialist groups prevented them from organizing a concerted attack on the country of the Soviets, and of course the mass of the people of England, France and the United States were exerting pressure on the governments of their countries, demanding from them a decisive rebuff of Fascism.

After Hitler's supporters came to power, Germany developed into the main hot-bed of a new world war. German Fascism was eager for world supremacy, starting with the enslavement of Europe. The plans of the Hitlerites envisaged the winning of 'living space' (*Lebensraum*) in the East, involving an armed advance against the Soviet Union under the false slogan of delivering Europe from the 'danger of Bolshevism'.

The intention of the German Fascists met with a sympathetic reception from the reactionary circles of the United States, England and France, who thought they could make use of Germany as a striking force of imperialism for the struggle against the Soviet Union and the democratic movement in Europe. The Hitlerites took steps to ensure that, in exchange, they would receive certain concessions from the Western States and, above all, a revision of the military clauses of the Versailles Treaty.

The Struggle of the Soviet Union for Peace and Collective Security

The only state to make an energetic effort to restrain the Fascist aggressors, to block the path to war and to uphold peace was the Soviet Union, which consistently maintained its anti-war policy. This won the sympathy of the mass of the people in foreign countries, thus spoiling the imperialist plans for war against the Soviet Union and forcing the governments of many states to review their relationship with the Soviet Union. In the years 1933 to 1935 more than ten countries, including the United States, established normal diplomatic relations with the Soviet Union. A clear indication of the increased international prestige of the USSR was its inclusion in the League of Nations in September, 1934, on the invitation of thirty states.

The Soviet Union attached great significance to solving the problem of disarmament. It proposed that the International Disarmament Conference should adopt the principle of complete disarmament, but the imperialists voted down not only this proposal, but even the Soviet draft for partial disarmament.

The Soviet Government considered it essential to use every means to contain the aggressors. From the tribune of the League of Nations, Soviet diplomacy, headed during these years by M. M. Litvinov, proclaimed the principle of 'Indivisible Peace'. Great popularity was achieved by the idea, put forward by the Soviet Union, of the creation of a system of security in Europe, whereby all states would combine to use their collective strength to deter aggression.

The Formation of the Fascist Bloc of States

The military and political collaboration of Germany and Italy at the time of their intervention in Spain hastened the formation of the bloc of Fascist states. In October, 1936, Germany and Italy signed an agreement to act in concert on basic questions of international politics and to fix their spheres of influence in central and south-east Europe.

At the same time a rapprochement occurred between Germany and Japan, interested in combining to forward their plans for aggression. In November, 1936, Germany and Japan concluded the so-called 'Anti-Comintern' pact which Italy joined a year later. The Fascist states made it their duty to inform each other of the activities of the Comintern* and to collaborate in fighting against it. A secret appendix contained the obligation not to conclude any political agreements with the Soviet Union which might contradict the pact, and to afford each other aid in case of war against the USSR.

The aggressive bloc of Berlin, Rome and Tokyo was created under the banner of the struggle against 'International Communism', but the real reason for the Fascist coalition lay in the desire of the monopolies of Germany, Italy and Japan to unleash war and thereby divide the world in their interests. The Soviet Union was not the only target for their aggression; the USA, England and France were also in the Fascists' sights. The chief role in the Fascist coalition was played by Hitler's Germany.

The Intensification of Fascist Aggression

After the conclusion of the 'Anti-Comintern' pact the aggression of the Fascist states became even more intense. In

---

* The International Communist Organization founded in Moscow in 1919; its aim was to encourage revolutionary forces throughout the world.

July, 1937, Japan invaded Northern China and began a broad-fronted advance into the depths of the country. This act threatened the interests of American and English imperialism in China, but the Governments of the United States and England turned a blind eye to the aggression and took no measures at all for the restoration of peace in the Far East. Washington and London hoped that Japan would soon attack the Soviet Union. The monopolies of the United States were supplying the Japanese imperialists with large quantities of metals, planes and oil-products, essential for the conduct of war.

New acts of aggression were committed by the Fascist states in Europe too. The first of these was the 'unification' of Austria with Germany (*Anschluss*), carried out under the pretext of uniting all the lands populated by Germans. Before taking this step, Hitler enlisted the support of the English Government, at the head of which stood the advocate of appeasement, N. Chamberlain.

The ruling circles of England, who regarded Germany as a 'bastion of the West against Bolshevism', gave it freedom of action in Central and Eastern Europe, and so, in March, 1938, the German Fascist troops marched into Austria, meeting no opposition. Austria ceased to exist as an independent state and became part of the German 'Reich'. England, France and the United States recognized this takeover.

The Soviet Union voiced firm criticism of the aggressive acts of Germany and proposed that an international conference should be summoned to guarantee the independence of those countries threatened by aggression. However, the Western Powers, having adopted the policy of bargaining with Hitler, once more rejected the Soviet Union's proposal.

The Munich Agreement

The fact that this aggression had gone unpunished encouraged Germany to make new conquests. The Hitlerites now gazed covetously at Czechoslovakia, which occupied an advantageous strategic position in the centre of Europe and whose industry was highly developed. The pretext for seizing the country was the German demand that Czechoslovakia should renounce her sovereignty over the Sudetenland—an integral part of the state, in which lived a German minority.

In the tense situation which had developed in the spring of 1938, the Governments of England and France informed the Czechs that they were not prepared to give them any military support and demanded their capitulation to Hitler. The United States fully supported this ultimatum.

The mass of the people of Czechoslovakia were in favour of a decisive rejection of the German claims and forced the Government to take certain defensive measures. The Soviet Union now raised its voice in defence of the independence of Czechoslovakia and peace in Europe. It informed the Government of Czechoslovakia that the Soviet Union was ready to go beyond the terms of the Soviet-Czechoslovak agreement and help Czechoslovakia without France, should such a request be made.

This agreement involving the Soviet Union, Czechoslovakia and France had provided for rapid support in case of an attack on one of the parties and had been signed in 1935. The Czech Government had stipulated that Soviet aid should be forthcoming only if France also came to the aid of the victim of attack. Nevertheless, the Soviet Government prepared to help Czechoslovakia by moving a large number of infantry and cavalry divisions, tank corps, armoured brigades and aircraft formations. These were soon ready for action.

In September, 1938, the Soviet Ambassador reported: 'In Prague, amazing scenes are happening. The Embassy is surrounded by a police cordon. In spite of this crowds of demonstrators, with the evident sympathy of the police, come to the door and ask to speak to me. The crowds are singing the National Anthem. They sing the "Internationale". Above all they want the Soviet Union to help . . . They want to fight to defend their country . . . summon Parliament and overthrow the Government. They want patriotic not defeatist speeches . . . Hitler and Chamberlain seem to arouse equal hatred.'

Despite the overwhelming feeling of the people, the bourgeois Government of Czechoslovakia would not accept help from the Soviet Union, even though the independence of the country was in peril. England and France then intensified their pressure, demanding that Czechoslovakia should accept Hitler's conditions and renounce its agreement with the Soviet Union. The Western Powers were worried lest Soviet help should hinder the seizure of Czechoslovakia by Hitler's Germany. Thus they hastened the preparation of an anti-Soviet agreement at Czechoslovakia's expense, trying to pass off this deal as 'the salvation of peace'.

On 29 and 30 September, 1938, in Munich, a conference brought together Chamberlain, Daladier, Hitler and Mussolini. A pact followed which increased the understanding between England, France and the Fascist Powers and which worked out in detail how Czechoslovakia was to be dismembered. The Sudeten and other frontier areas of the country were handed over to Germany. The Czech Government offered no resistance, although, when fully mobilized, Czechoslovakia had under arms seventy divisions compared to fifty-two German. The rulers of Czechoslovakia accepted the Munich Agreement, having already started on the path of betraying the nation.

The United States, having played an off-stage role in the organization of the Munich Agreement, approved its results.

By handing over Czechoslovakia to Hitler, the ruling circles of England and France hoped that he had received sufficient payment to renounce aggression in Western Europe and that now he would surely start a war against the Soviet Union. The imperialist strategists had miscalculated. The Munich Agreement marked the high point of the Western Powers' policy of encouraging Fascist aggression in the hope of turning it against the Soviet Union. Their leaders' triumph roused boundless appetites in the Hitlerites and in March, 1939, Germany seized the remaining part of Czechoslovakia. Bohemia and Moravia became German 'protectorates', and a puppet government was created in 'independent' Slovakia.

Anglo-Franco-Soviet Discussions

The alignment of forces in Europe had changed to the advantage of the Fascist states. The aggravation of the deep-rooted conflict of interests between the two imperialist groups made open war between them more certain.

In March, 1939, Germany seized the port of Memel belonging to Lithuania. Having begun preparations for an attack on Poland, Hitler demanded that Danzig should be handed over to Germany. In April the Italian Fascists occupied Albania.

These new seizures in Europe forced the Western Powers to change their tactics in carrying out their previous Munich policy.

In order to obtain particular advantages in trade with Hitler, England and France took certain measures to strengthen their military-political position. Their parliaments ratified large military budgets. The Western Powers gave the assurance of aid to a number of European countries, including Poland, in case of an attack upon them. In the spring of 1939 England and France were obliged to enter into negotiations with the Soviet Union regarding common action against aggressors.

The Soviet Government tried to achieve the successful conclusion of a military agreement and of a tripartite pact of mutual aid in case of aggression. The Soviet Union considered it essential to define precisely the extent of this aid, and also to include in any agreement the obligation to defend a number of other countries in Eastern and Western Europe, which were threatened by Fascist aggression.

Reactionary historians allege that the Soviet Union did not make sufficient effort to conclude a military agreement with England and France. The facts, however, speak otherwise. The Governments of Chamberlain and Daladier refused to accept a treaty based on principles of equality and reciprocity. They wanted to bind the Soviet Union with the type of obligation that would inevitably lead it into war with Germany; the Soviet Union would also have been deprived of reliable Anglo-French guarantees. When, after long delays, in August, 1939, military missions from England and France arrived in Moscow, it became clear that they had not even the authority to sign a military convention. Through the fault of the Western Powers the negotiations reached deadlock and were broken off.

At the same time in London the English Government was carrying on secret negotiations for a new agreement with Hitler concerning the Soviet Union and the other countries of Eastern Europe.

The Soviet-German Non-Aggression Pact

By August, 1939, the international position of the Soviet Union had run into serious complications. Germany was preparing to attack Poland. The provocations of the Japanese militarists had become more frequent; they were undertaking military adventures on the far-eastern frontiers of the Soviet Union. The Soviet Union was now faced with the prospect of international isolation and involvement in war in both the west and the east.

At that time Germany proposed to the Soviet Government

the signing of a ten-year non-aggression pact. The acceptance of the German proposition enabled the Soviet Union to avoid war on two fronts in unfavourable conditions, and to gain time to strengthen the country's defences. The treaty made it possible to stave off the creation of the united anti-Soviet front which was being prepared by the imperialist states.

The Soviet Union accepted the German proposal, and on 23 August, 1939, the non-aggression treaty was signed. The perfidious politics of the Western Powers forced the Soviet Union to take this step. The Soviet Government realized that Hitler had not given up his plans for war against the Soviet Union, and that his proposal was a routine manœuvre of the Fascist leadership. History has upheld the correctness of the decision that was taken. The men of Munich had not succeeded in pushing the Soviet Union into conflict with the Fascist states while themselves remaining on the side-lines.

Skilfully taking advantage of the inter-imperialist contradictions, the Soviet Union had prevented an anti-Soviet agreement between the two groups. The Hitlerites then came to the conclusion that victory in the west would be easier than in the east. Their aim was to consolidate their rear, to mobilize all the anti-Soviet forces and the resources of Europe, and then to hurl them against the Soviet Union.

The Second World War began with an armed skirmish of the two imperialist coalitions. In its origins this war was an imperialist one. It was the aggressive bloc of Fascist states headed by Hitlerite Germany which unleashed the war. It is they who must bear the blame for this totally unjustified war which, on the Fascist side, had nothing but predatory aims from start to finish.

CHAPTER II

$\star$

The Start of the Second World War

$\star$

The Invasion of Poland

On 1 September, 1939, German troops invaded Poland. England and France, having promised aid to Poland, declared war on Germany on 3 September. In reply Hitler said, 'It still doesn't mean that they will really fight.' And indeed, England and France betrayed Poland just as they had previously betrayed Czechoslovakia. One hundred and fifteen French and English divisions stood idle, while they had facing them, at most, twenty-three German divisions. The ruling circles of the Western Powers expected that, when they had defeated Poland, Germany would move against the Soviet Union. After the Hitlerian invasion the Polish Government and the army leaders shamefully fled abroad, leaving the nation to the whims of fate. Many army regiments and also the population of Warsaw and other towns fought heroically against the enemy. The workers, rallying round the Communists, fought in the first ranks of the defenders of Polish soil. But the balance of military power was on the side of the Hitlerites. It took the Fascist hordes about three weeks to crush the resistance of the disorganized Polish army and to occupy a significant part of the country.

The Hitlerian advance towards the east not only threatened the Soviet Union, but it also meant slavery for the population of the Western Ukraine and Western Byelorussia. To counter this possibility and because these territories had been illegally included in the composition of Poland in 1920, the Soviet Union took under its protection the life and property of the Western Ukrainians and Western Byelorussians.

When the war in Europe began, the United States declared its neutrality. The American monopolists calculated that the war would bring the economy of the country out of crisis, and that the orders for munitions placed by the warring powers would bring huge profits to the industrialists and bankers.

After the defeat of Poland, England and France still hoped for an agreement with Hitler, in order to direct Fascist aggression against the Soviet Union.

The Armed Conflict with Finland

The Second World War was spreading ever further. The Soviet state was faced with the acute problem of further strengthening its security, in particular on the frontier with Finland. At that time the Soviet-Finnish border passed 32 kilometres from Leningrad.* On the isthmus of Karelia, Finland, with the help of the large imperialist states, had constructed huge fortifications, thus creating a military spring-board for an attack on the USSR. The Finnish Government declined the invitation of the USSR to conclude a mutual aid agreement and broke off negotiations concerning the exchange of Finnish territory near Leningrad for twice as much territory in Karelia. At the end of November, 1939, artillery fire directed in provocation against our territory from the Finnish side forced the Soviet Government to take retaliatory measures.

Thus Finnish reactionary forces, incited by Fascist Germany and the other imperialist powers, unleashed war

* See Map, p. 116.

against the Soviet Union. The Finnish military command had thought they could hold the Soviet troops on the approaches to the so-called 'Mannerheim Line', consisting of a system of huge fortifications, and then, when they had received aid from the Western Powers, they hoped to pass to the attack and transfer military operations on to the territory of the USSR.

Anti-Soviet circles in the USA, England and France were overjoyed at the news that hostilities had broken out, expecting that this would mean the beginning of a great war.

England and France had sent a large quantity of war materials into Finland. The Governments of these countries were preparing to despatch to Finland an expeditionary force numbering 150,000. At the same time they were evolving plans for launching an attack from the airfields of Syria on the Soviet oilfields in Baku. The USA lent Finland ten million dollars and gave them 10,000 rifles. Finland also received weapons from Germany and Italy.

The Red Army offensive on the Karelian isthmus began on 11 February, 1940. Over a period of twenty days fierce battles took place, the 'Mannerheim Line' was breached and the armed forces of Finland defeated.

Having suffered defeat, the Finnish militarists sued for peace. On 12 March, 1940, in Moscow, a peace treaty was signed in which Finland agreed to move its frontier to follow a line along the Karelian isthmus, north-west of Lake Ladoga. They also agreed to lease the Hangö peninsula to the Soviet Union. In signing the peace treaty with Finland, the Soviet Union limited itself to making the minimum demands consistent with the security of our north-west frontier.

Thus the defeat of the Finnish troops and the conclusion of a peace treaty between the Soviet Union and Finland in March, 1940, spoilt the plans for the organization of a 'great crusade' of world imperialism against the Soviet Union.

The 'Phoney War'

For seven months there was no military activity on the Western Front. The war got the ironic nickname of 'phoney war'. The resources of England and France were superior to the military economic potential of Germany, which at that time was not ready for a prolonged war. But the Governments of England and France, still keeping to their Munich policy, gave Hitler to understand that he would have a free hand in the east. Instead of making war on Germany, the French ruling circles concentrated on suppressing the progressive forces of the country, in particular the Communist Party which then had to go underground.

Meanwhile Germany, taking advantage of the inactivity of the Allies, was steadily preparing to attack on the Western Front.

The Fall of France

In April, 1940, the Hitlerites suddenly invaded Denmark and Norway and quickly occupied them. They met with no resistance from the Danish army, as the King and Government ordered the troops to lay down their arms. The Norwegian patriots put up a valiant resistance, inflicting heavy losses on the German aggressors. But at the beginning of June the Norwegian army's resistance was broken. This was brought about to a significant extent by the 'fifth column', consisting of local Fascists.

The fact that Hitler had first of all attacked in the west proved conclusively the complete failure of the Munich policy. National indignation forced the resignation of N. Chamberlain, the ring-leader of the English 'men of Munich'. The new Government was headed by a more flexible statesman of the Conservative party, Winston Churchill, who understood the nature of the danger hanging over England.

Winston Churchill (1874–1965) came from an aristocratic family, the lords of Marlborough. He took part in the colonial wars. He twice changed his political party, going from the Conservatives to the Liberals and back again. Churchill, whom Lenin called the 'chief hater of Soviet Russia', was a stubborn enemy of the social and national emancipation of the nations, and an ardent defender of capitalism.

In May the German Fascist troops seized the Netherlands, Belgium and Luxembourg. Skirting from the north the Maginot Line, a line of defences constructed by the French along the frontier with Germany, the Hitlerites broke through the front and advanced towards the coast. The English troops, about 340,000 in number, were driven back to the sea at Dunkirk. Abandoning their military equipment they were evacuated to the British Isles. The Dunkirk 'miracle' can be explained by the fact that Hitler forbade his generals to annihilate the English, in the expectation that he could make temporary peace with them and safeguard his rear to the west.

On 5 June the Hitler troops began an offensive towards the south, threatening Paris. The French nation and army were filled with resolve to fight the enemy. The Communists demanded that a home guard should be created and that a national war should be waged for freedom and national independence. But the Government of industrialists and bankers betrayed the national interests of France. It was afraid to arm the workers for the struggle against the attackers, preferring to abandon all resistance and flee from the capital. Paris, declared an 'open city', was surrendered to the Hitler troops without a fight. The defeatist policy of the ruling circles had a demoralizing influence on the army.

At the head of the new Government stood one of the leaders of the French Fascists—Marshal Pétain. On 22 June, 1940, in the Forest of Compiègne France signed the act of capitulation. In order to humiliate France, the Hitlerites made her representatives sign this shameful document in the very railway coach where in 1918 Marshal Foch dictated the conditions of the armistice to the German delegation. Most of France was occupied. In the southern, unoccupied part of the country, the military Fascist régime of Pétain's puppet government was established, based in the spa of Vichy.

Only a few individuals among the bourgeoisie and higher-ranking officers stood out against the capitulators. Among them was General Charles de Gaulle (1890–1970). From London, he appealed to French servicemen stationed overseas, and many patriots joined the 'Free French' movement to fight for the rebirth of their native land.

The Gradual Involvement of the USA in the War

The seizure of Western Europe by the Hitlerites provoked disquiet in the United States. The American Government implemented a large-scale programme of military construction and increased the size of the armed forces. Work began on the creation of the atomic bomb. Already in the autumn of 1939 the law concerning 'neutrality' had been altered, and the belligerent states had had the opportunity to obtain munitions and war materials from the United States on condition they were paid for in cash and exported on the purchasers' own ships. Although not involved in the war, the United States afforded England ever-growing military and economic aid. In March, 1941, Congress passed the Lend-Lease Act, that is the lending or leasing of armaments and war materials to those countries whose defence against aggression had a vitally important significance for the United States. This meant that the United States of America wished to defend its own security above all by the efforts of England and other countries waging war with the munitions and war materials received from America.

In June, 1940, Italy entered the war. In September her troops began an offensive in North Africa. They advanced in an easterly direction with the aim of seizing Egypt and establishing control over the Suez Canal. The Italian army also broadened the area which they had occupied in East Africa. But the invaders' mastery of this area turned out to be short-lived. As a result of an offensive by British troops Italy was soon deprived of her possessions in East Africa.

On receiving reinforcements the British drove the invaders out of Egypt and defeated the Italian army in Cyrenaica. Then German troops came to the aid of their Italian allies. In the spring of 1941 the Fascists began an offensive in Libya, occupied Benghazi and surrounded Tobruk. However, their advance inside the boundaries of Egypt itself was halted. The Hitler troops had no reserves for offensive operations in the African continent, as they were gathering their forces together for waging war on the Soviet Union.

CHAPTER III

$\star$

The Preparation for War Against the USSR

$\star$

After the fall of France Hitler decided that the time had come for an attack on the USSR. Now the whole of Fascist Germany's policy was subordinated to the preparations for war against the Soviet Union.

The Fascist Attacks on England and in the Balkans

Concealing their preparation for invading the Soviet Union, the Fascists began their barbarous air raids of English towns. The German High Command more than once postponed the date of their invasion of the British Isles, and then put off the landings for an indefinite period. Hitler had come to the conclusion that, in the case of a victory over the Soviet Union, England would be brought to her knees without any great effort. As was proved by later events, the decisive force which saved England from Fascist enslavement was the Soviet Union.

Preparing for the attack on the USSR, Hitler's Germany established control over the countries of South-East Europe. In October, 1940, German troops entered Rumania, where the Fascist dictatorship of General Antonescu* had become

* Ion Antonescu (1882–1946). Pro-German dictator of the country from September, 1940. Sentenced to death as a war criminal.

firmly established. The Nazis subjugated Hungary, which was under the rule of the Fascist régime of the dictator Horthy.

In March, 1941, the Hitlerites led their troops into Bulgaria, which they had included in their aggressive bloc.

In April, 1941, Yugoslavia and Greece were occupied and dismembered. The countries of South-East Europe were forcibly transformed into a platform for an attack on the Soviet Union.

The Gradual Change in the Character of the Second World War

In those countries occupied by the Fascists there existed a reign of blood and terror. The Hitlerites destroyed the national independence of the peoples. In order to terrify the masses the Fascists brought in a system of hostages. Where the population proved intransigent or where partisans became active the Hitlerites threw into prison and killed thousands of people.

Occupied Europe was covered with a network of death camps. In one such camp alone in Poland more than four million people were annihilated during the war years.

The Hitlerites introduced forced labour. They made workers toil for the invaders for an insignificant wage. Millions of people were forcibly sent off to work in Germany. The Hitlerites plundered the occupied countries, taking away a huge quantity of raw materials and supplies.

But the Fascists did not manage to extinguish the burning desire for freedom and independence. The masses rose in a struggle for justice and freedom against the hated invaders. In Czechoslovakia, Poland, France, Yugoslavia, Albania and other enslaved countries Resistance Movements grew up.

Everywhere it was the Communists who were the organizers of the anti-Fascist struggle. Under their direction the patriots carried out sabotage, attacked the invaders and created companies of partisans. Workers organized strikes and sabotaged factories to prevent them fulfilling German orders.

In May, 1941, Manolis Glezoss, a valiant son of the Greek people, carried out a heroic exploit. Risking his life, the 19-year-old patriot tore the Fascist flag with the swastika from the Acropolis in Athens. From that moment an extensive resistance movement began to spread through Greece.

From the very beginning, the Second World War showed signs of becoming a war for justice and freedom. For the states which were in conflict with the Hitler bloc the war became more and more an anti-Fascist one. The struggle of Western Powers against the aggressor countries began to combine with the just fight of the enslaved peoples of Europe and Asia for national independence, freedom and democracy. Thus from the second half of 1940 onwards, the war, starting as a conflict between two groups of imperialist states, turned into a fight for justice and freedom.

In the spring of 1941 almost all the continent of Europe had been overrun by the Hitler troops. The huge resources of the occupied countries, both in men and materials, were now at the disposition of the German aggressors. Over the Soviet Union there hung a direct threat of Fascist invasion.

CHAPTER IV

★

The Soviet Economy and the State of the Armed Forces on the Eve of the Great Patriotic War

★

The USSR—A Mighty Industrial Power

By successfully carrying out the five-year plans, the Soviet people had transformed their country into a mighty industrial and agricultural power. On the basis of its industrial output, the Soviet Union now occupied first place in Europe and second place in the world (after the USA). In the pre-war years, 9,000 large industrial concerns were constructed, most of them in the field of heavy industry. Huge industrial centres were created in the east of the country.

In 1940 the gross output of all our industry was 8·5 times greater than the industrial production of Czarist Russia in 1913. In the course of this period the output of large-scale industry increased 12-fold and machine-building 35-fold. Together with industrialization, an important role in increasing the defence potential of the country was played by the Socialist transformation of agriculture, which allowed the Soviet State in the main to guarantee the supplies of food for its population, and of raw materials for industry, and enabled significant stocks of raw materials and food to be built up in the pre-war years.

However, agriculture went through periods of great

difficulty. The gross yield of grain in 1940 reached 5,830 million poods* at the most; that is, only slightly more than in 1913. Cattle-breeding was developing slowly.

Measures Taken to Increase the Defence Potential of the Country

On the basis of industrialization the USSR had created a modern defence industry which developed especially fast in the pre-war years.

In 1939–40 Soviet scientists and construction engineers developed striking examples of new military equipment, and industry put them into production.

The Air Force began to receive new types of fighter planes, the MiG 3, Lagg 3, Yak 1 fighters, the Stormovik dive bombers and the IL2 and PE2 bombers. New tanks and artillery were designed and industry began to produce the famous T34 tanks, field guns and howitzers which surpassed all (including German types) in their tactical and technical qualities. On the eve of the war, our military scientists invented multi-rail rocket projectors which subsequently became very popular with the troops—the famous 'Katyushas'.

The defence industry turned out more planes, tanks and other military equipment than Germany; yet the most recent types were not being produced in sufficient quantity. The production of war material by Soviet industry was far from reaching its full capacity.

In the pre-war years great attention was paid to increasing State reserves—stocks of raw materials, fuel, metals and food laid up in case of war.

Because of the growing threat of war, the Soviet state drafted new guidelines to industry in order to further strengthen the country's defence capacity. In 1940 the Praesidium of the Supreme Soviet of the USSR issued the

* 1 pood = 18 kilos.

decree announcing the change to an eight-hour working day and a seven-day working week. Up to June, 1940, the so-called 'six-day week' (five working days, one day off) had been in force. The decree also prohibited workers from leaving their jobs unless so directed.

This decree met with wide support from the workers. In all State enterprises working discipline was strengthened, productivity was raised and output of goods essential for the defence of the country was increased.

In 1940, with the aim of systematically training a qualified working force for the main branches of the national economy, a broad network of special schools was created. Schools in factories, craft schools, railway training centres were set up which every year trained about a million young people from town and country.

In September, 1939, the Supreme Soviet of the USSR, in response to Article 132 of the Constitution, which had pronounced the defence of the Fatherland to be the sacred duty of each of its citizens, passed a new law 'Concerning General Military Service', which guaranteed the increase in numbers of the armed forces and created better conditions for the soldiers of the Red Army to master complicated military equipment.

The Communist Party, the Soviet Government and the whole of our nation has always paid great attention to the strengthening of the Armed Forces of our country. By June, 1941, the Red Army had reached a total of 4,207,000. Between 1939 and 1941 the Soviet Air Force had grown more than twofold. However, many military units were still at the stage of assembling men and equipment. They were just starting their instruction and the new military machines were only just being brought into service.

In the units and sub-units of the Red Army, political work was intensified. On the day of the twenty-first anniversary of the Soviet Armed Forces all those engaged in military service took a new military oath: 'I am always prepared', solemnly swore the Soviet soldiers, 'at the command of the worker-peasant Government to go to the defence of my Fatherland—the Union of Soviet Socialist Republics, and, as a soldier of the Worker-Peasant Army, I swear to defend it valiantly, efficiently, with dignity and honour, not sparing my blood and my very life to achieve complete victory over our enemies.'

The Red Army Command had gained experience from the battles fought in the Soviet-Finnish war and they were attentively studying the military operations that had begun in Europe. All this helped to prepare the Soviet Armed Forces to wage a modern war.

However, the work undertaken to increase the size of the Red Army, to rearm it and to improve its combat efficiency was to remain uncompleted by the beginning of the Great Patriotic War.

CHAPTER V

★

The Start of the Great Patriotic War

✗

The Perfidious Attack of Fascist Germany

Early on the morning of 22 June, 1941, Fascist Germany treacherously attacked the Soviet Union. Hitler threw into the attack 190 divisions and an enormous number of tanks and aircraft. Together with the Hitler invaders, Italian, Finnish, Rumanian and Hungarian troops advanced onto Soviet soil.

In the very first hours of the war the enemy launched massive air raids. Fascist planes dropped bombs on Soviet towns, aerodromes and railway junctions. Thousands of guns opened fire on the frontier posts and at the areas where units of the Red Army were stationed. Shock formations of enemy tanks and motorized convoys burst onto Soviet soil.

It was only after an hour and a half of the start of military operations that the German Consul in Moscow informed the Soviet Government that Germany considered herself to be in a state of war with the Soviet Union. Thus did Fascist Germany, flagrantly breaking the Soviet-German non-aggression pact, treacherously unleash war against the USSR.

To prepare for the attack on our country, the Hitlerites devised in 1940 the so-called 'Barbarossa' plan. It provided for the launching of a 'lightning war' (*Blitzkrieg*), the defeat of the Red Army, the capture of Moscow and the advance of the German troops in the course of eight weeks to a line stretching from Archangel to Astrakhan.

The Hitlerites wished to annihilate the first socialist state in the world, to break our country up into a string of separate states dependent on Germany, to exterminate many millions of Soviet citizens, and to turn those who remained alive into their slaves.

The war which Fascist Germany had undertaken against the Soviet Union was a war inspired by imperialism and its policies of expansion and extortion. The predatory character of the war and the long-standing unbridled Fascist propaganda had transformed the German army into an army of murderers, robbers and oppressors, deprived of any moral principles.

The Soviet nation, under the leadership of the Communist party, embarked upon a Great Patriotic War against the Fascist invaders.

In this war our nation had as its aim the defence of honour, freedom and the independence of our Socialist Fatherland, the destruction of the Fascist invaders, and the provision of help to the nations of Europe so that they might free themselves from the bloody Fascist yoke. The high and noble aims of the Patriotic War inspired the Soviet people to boundless exploits, and gave birth to the mass heroism of the whole nation such as never before seen in history.

The Forced Retreat of the Red Army in the Early Period of the War

From the very first hours of battle the Soviet troops along the whole extent of the Soviet-German frontier, from the Black Sea to the Barents Sea, offered heroic resistance to the enemy. The regular units of the Red Army and the border guards fought with exceptional bravery and valour.

A small garrison of the legendary Brest [Litovsk] fortress, though surrounded, beat off furious enemy attacks for more than a month. Resistance ceased only when not one of the fortress's defenders remained. 'I am dying but will not surrender. Farewell, my country! 20.VII.1941.' This inscription was made by an unknown hero, one of the last defenders of the Brest fortress.

On 26 June, 1941, pilot Nikolai Gastello performed a deathless exploit. He flew his plane, which had been shot down and was on fire, directly at a crowd of enemy lorries and fuel tanks. The Fascists paid a high price for the death of the heroic Soviet pilot. Dozens of German lorries flew up into the air. For this exploit Captain Gastello was posthumously awarded the title of 'Hero of the Soviet Union'.

The front-line units of the Red Army waged war under the most difficult conditions. The Fascist troops, taking advantage of their superiority in men and equipment, inflicted heavy losses on our units. Shock formations of tanks and motorized convoys drove around the flanks of the Soviet troops and penetrated deep into the rear. Concerted action between the various formations of the Red Army was rendered impossible. Many units continued to fight even under conditions of complete encirclement. Therefore, in spite of all its valour and bravery, the Red Army was forced to retreat. By the beginning of July the enemy had seized Lithuania, a significant part of Latvia, the Western Ukraine, Western Byelorussia and part of Moldavia. The threat of mortal danger hung over our socialist Fatherland.

Why had this happened? Up to the moment of its attack on the Soviet Union the economy of Fascist Germany had been fully directed towards war-production. Besides this, Germany had at its disposal the resources of those European countries which it had already occupied. Thus it was that, in the early days, the Fascist army had numerical superiority in military equipment over the Soviet Union, and in certain classes of weapon they also had qualitative superiority. As for the economy of the Soviet Union, it had been subordinated to the interests of peaceful reconstruction, and

27

although there did exist large industries turning out military equipment, mass-production of the more perfected forms of weapon was only just getting under way.

The German Fascist troops were fully mobilized and had experience of military operations over the previous two years. By the time they attacked the Soviet Union, the Fascist command had concentrated near our frontiers a huge invasion force of seasoned troops. Germany attacked the Soviet Union after gaining decisive victories in the west. Therefore Hitler could throw into the attack an overwhelming number of his armed forces. Other countries fought with Germany against the Soviet Union: Italy, Finland, Rumania and Hungary, where reactionary Fascist governments were in power. Besides this, Fascist Germany was given aid by Japan, Spain, Bulgaria and Turkey. In the beginning the Soviet Union and its Red Army had to fight alone against Germany and its allies. The Soviet command, fearing a sudden attack on the part of Japan, was forced to maintain large armed forces in the Far East, and also on the frontiers of the Caucasus in order to repulse a possible attack by Turkey.

The really serious military advantage enjoyed by Germany consisted in the fact that she had begun the war against our country so abruptly. Naturally, the attack of the German invaders was not completely unexpected by the Soviet Union. The Communist Party and the Soviet Government knew that in spite of the non-aggression pact, Germany would start a war against the USSR. So the country and army were ready to defend themselves. A plan for mobilization had been worked out and put into action, providing for the placing of industry on a war footing, and the transfer of troops from the interior of the country to the Western frontiers had already begun. New army formations were being set up. The Red Army was being equipped with the newest war materials. But the country had not completed its defence preparations, and this fact predetermined our temporary lack of success in the early stages of the war.

World Reaction to the Fascist Attack

The brigand-like advance of the German Fascist troops into the Soviet Union was greeted particularly by the reactionary circles of the United States and England with undisguised delight. They thought that as a result of the war the USSR would be bled white and would become dependent on the Western Powers. The very day after Germany's attack on the Soviet Union, one of the American reactionaries, Senator H. Truman (later on to be President of the United States) declared: 'If we see Germany winning, then we should help Russia, and if Russia is winning, we should help Germany; so that in that way as many as possible should be killed.'

Quite different, however, was the reaction of the broad masses of the people to the aggression against the Soviet Union. They saw that the Soviet Union had the power to destroy the war machine of Hitler's Germany and to save world civilization from Fascist barbarism. The people of the United States, England and the other capitalist countries came out in favour of supplying aid to the Soviet Union.

The most far-seeing politicians among the English and American bourgeoisie realized that collaboration with the USSR was essential to their own interests. They were convinced that the Fascist aggressors threatened the existence of the British Empire and the security of the United States. In July, 1941, the USA and England met and agreed on combined action in the war against Germany. At the Moscow three-power conference, involving the USSR, the USA and England, which took place from 29 September to 1 October, 1941, a decision was taken about the supply of Anglo-American arms and strategic materials to the Soviet Union over the following nine months. In its turn, the Soviet Union pledged itself to supply the United States and England with raw materials for war production. Soon the United States Government gave the Soviet Union credit to the amount of one thousand million dollars and extended the Lend-Lease Act to include the Soviet Union.

Thus in 1941 the basis for the creation of an anti-Fascist coalition was laid down. But the supplies of munitions and war materials made to the Soviet Union by the Allies were irregular, deliveries suffered long delays and in the first year of the war they had little practical significance for the Soviet Union.

The Mobilization of the Soviet People for the Struggle with the Enemy

With enormous patriotic fervour, and with uncrushable faith in victory over the enemy, the Soviet people rose up to wage the Great Patriotic War. 'We place ourselves at the disposition of the Communist Party and the Soviet Government and will fight to the last drop of blood for our country' declared the workers at a meeting of the Leningrad factory named after A. A. Zhdanov.

On 22 June, 1941, general mobilization was declared and the European part of the Soviet Union put on a war footing. Besides the conscripts, hundreds of thousands of volunteers went to the call-up points, begging to be sent to the front.

On 29 June, 1941, the Central Committee of the Communist party and the Council of People's Commissars of the USSR addressed a directive to the party and council organizations in the districts near the front line. This set out a programme for the mobilization of all the forces of the country in the fight against the enemy. The party and the Government called on the Soviet people to recognize the extreme peril threatening the country, to reorganize all their work on a war footing, to organize comprehensive assistance for those at the front, to increase war-production in all ways possible, and in the case of the Red Army's being forced to retreat, to carry off or destroy all valuable property and to wage guerrilla warfare behind the enemy's lines.

On 30 June the State Committee for Defence was formed with J. V. Stalin as chairman. The powers of the state were completely concentrated in the hands of this committee.

The Central Committee sent many prominent members of the party and of the Soviet Government into the most important fields of war-production and farm-work. The party mobilized and sent to the front those Communists and members of the Komsomol* who were best prepared for war. By the end of 1941 1,300,000 Communists and more than two million members of the Komsomol were fighting in the army. Every activity of state, economic and social organizations was subordinated to the needs of the front. In a short time most enterprises were ready for war-production. From the early days of the war, patriotic fervour developed everywhere and people took to heart the slogan: 'Work twice as hard; work to replace your comrade who has gone to the front.' Hundreds of thousands worked shifts to fulfil two or three daily quotas each. The number of machine operatives sharply increased, and it became common practice for one person to do more than one job.

On the workshop floor women and young people came to replace the men who had gone to the front, and pensioners returned to work. Women took over jobs previously done by men; they learnt how to temper steel, forge iron, and handle the most complicated machinery. Those who had left school only the day before successfully learnt how to carry out complicated production processes. And yet there were not enough hands in the work-force. This is why for the duration

* Communist Youth League, set up in 1918 to assist the Communist Party.

of the war an eleven-hour working day was established and annual holidays cancelled.

In September, 1941, the members of the Komsomol employed in a motor-works formed themselves into a 'Komsomol-Youth Front-Line Brigade' and soon others in factories throughout the country followed their initiative, and fulfilled double the normal work quota.

More than ten million people from those areas immediately threatened by the enemy invasion were evacuated to the Urals, Western Siberia, Kazakhstan, and the republics of Central Asia. 1,563 large industrial concerns of paramount importance for the defence of the country were also moved to those areas. These factories were re-established in a very short time in their new homes. People worked tirelessly day and night, out in the open, in rain and snow, in order to get the factories stripped as fast as possible. The workmen lived on a meagre diet in dug-outs and tents. The effort and heroism put into their work by the Soviet people and the party organizations brought unprecedented results: the factory installation took only three to four weeks, and in a few months most of the evacuated factories had reached their pre-war level of production.

However, in the second half of 1941, owing to the loss of a number of important industrial areas, output was more than halved taking the country as a whole. This was the most difficult period in the development of the wartime economy.

From the autumn of 1941 the whole burden of providing bread and provisions for those at home and those at the front lay on the eastern provinces. Since the men had gone into the army all the work in agriculture had lain on the shoulders of women, adolescents and old men. There was a shortage of fuel for tractors and combine-harvesters. But even in these difficult conditions the 1941 harvest was completely gathered in.

In the summer and autumn of 1941 the Red Army fought fierce defensive battles against the invading forces of Nazi Germany. The Smolensk battle lasted almost two months. The enemy was held at this point until the middle of September. The German invaders suffered enormous losses and were forced to postpone for more than a month their attack on Moscow.

At the beginning of September the Hitlerites broke through towards Leningrad, and blockaded it from the land side, but in spite of their great numerical advantage, they could not achieve any decisive success. The Soviet troops remained unshakeable. The People's Volunteer Corps, numbering more than 160,000, came to their aid. Communists and members of the Komsomol made up as much as 40 per cent of the People's Volunteer Corps. Hundreds of thousands of the inhabitants constructed fortifications on the approaches to the town and in its streets. The sailors of the Baltic fleet played a large role in the defence of Leningrad, by preventing the enemy from approaching from the Gulf of Finland, and by subjecting the land forces to heavy artillery fire.

The enemy came up against an indestructible line o defences and proceeded to besiege Leningrad, hoping to break the will of its citizens by ceaseless bombardments and artillery fire, and subdue them with the bony hand of hunger.

The heroic defence of Kiev lasted more than two months, from the beginning of July until 19 September. 160,000 of its citizens raised defensive barriers along the approaches to the city. On these lines of defence, units of the Red Army and the People's Volunteer Corps halted the advance of the German Fascist forces. The Soviet soldiers fought valiantly to their last breath.

The following note was found with the Komsomol

membership card of the infantry soldier A. Cobolev, who died a heroic death, 'Let the enemy realize that the soldiers of the Red Army will not allow themselves to be taken prisoner; if necessary they will die instead, but they will die only a hero's death. I have already eliminated from the enemy ranks no fewer than twenty Fascists and I will go on fighting for the Fatherland, shedding my blood drop by drop. If I have to die, then I will die fighting, convinced that Fascism will be destroyed and that victory will be ours.'

The Hitlerites lost more than 100,000 officers and men at the approaches to Kiev. Only when they brought up fresh forces did they manage to break through the front south-east of Kiev. Threatened with encirclement, the units of the Red Army were forced to leave the city.

The heroic defence of Odessa lasted from 4 August to 16 October—seventy-three days. Completely blockaded from the land, units of the Red Marines, supported by the Black Sea fleet and the inhabitants of the town, withstood the onslaught of eighteen enemy divisions. In the battle for Odessa the German and Rumanian troops lost more than 110,000 soldiers and a large quantity of equipment.

The stubborn resistance of the heroic cities of Leningrad, Kiev and Odessa and the defensive battle at Smolensk played an important role in frustrating the Hitler plan for a 'lightning war'.

The Soviet Troops Foil the Enemy Plans to Capture Moscow

As they had a significant advantage, especially in their numbers of tanks and aircraft, the Fascist command decided to attack from the north and the south, while at the same time delivering a severe blow from the west. By these means they hoped to surround and annihilate the Soviet troops and capture Moscow. At the end of September, seventy-five enemy divisions began a general offensive against Moscow.

The troops of the Red Army barred their path, and at the approaches to the Soviet capital a bitter fight began.

On 19 October the State Committee for Defence announced that Moscow was in a state of siege. In response to an appeal by the Moscow committee of the party, hundreds of thousands of Muscovites came forward to build defence works. On the outskirts of the capital city they made anti-tank ditches, scarps, trenches, barbed-wire entanglements, and hundreds of kilometres of timber barriers. The streets of Moscow were blocked with barricades, anti-tank barriers and metal 'hedgehogs'.

In the factories work went on ceaselessly by day and night to produce weapons, ammunition and equipment. Hundreds of thousands of Muscovites joined the ranks of the People's Volunteer Corps and fighting battalions. More than 100,000 Communists and 200,000 members of the Komsomol had left Moscow for the front.

The troops of the Red Army withstood heavy attacks from the German Fascist invaders and halted them to the north of Kalinin, to the west of Mozhaysk and at the approaches to Tula.

At this time fraught with danger, Moscow, now in the front line, observed the twenty-fourth anniversary of the October Revolution. On 6 November, 1941, a solemn session of the Moscow Council took place in the Mayakovsky metro station. This meeting was also attended by party organizations and social groups in the capital, and on the following day troops from the Moscow Garrison paraded in Red Square. The troops, armed for battle, marched past Lenin's Mausoleum, and went straight from the parade to the front.

On 15 November, 1941, the Hitlerites began their second 'general attack' on Moscow. The enemy did not expect to suffer any great losses and so rushed headlong into the attack. On 25 November Fascist troops occupied Klin and reached the Moscow–Volga canal in the area around Yakhroma. Boundless heroism was demanded of the Soviet soldiers who had the task of halting the enemy. Our troops fought with exceptional bravery. The nearer they came to Moscow, the harder did our troops fight to defend the city. The German divisions suffered ever greater losses and were forced to bring up their last reinforcements.

In order to stop the enemy throwing reserves from other sections of the front into the Moscow battle, the Red Army command started offensive operations in the Rostov and Tikhvin areas.

In the western parts of the Moscow region, which were already occupied by the enemy, dozens of partisan units carried on the struggle; thousands of Komsomol members fought valiantly in the ranks of the partisans, and many of them gave their lives for their country.

At some points the Hitlerites managed to get as near as twenty-five or thirty kilometres from Moscow, but they could not break through the Soviet lines. The enemy was halted at the approaches to the capital. Up to half their fighting strength had been lost or killed and wounded.

The Heroic Defence of Leningrad in the Winter of 1941–42

At the same time as they were attacking Moscow, the Hitlerites were making a determined attempt to capture Leningrad. The city was blockaded on all sides by enemy troops. The heroic inhabitants went on turning out tanks, weapons, ammunition and equipment for the Red Army units which were defending the city. Many thousands of workers from factories and offices joined the People's Volunteer Force and heroically defended their native city.

In their frenzied malice the enemy daily subjected Leningrad to air raids and barbaric artillery fire, killing old men, women and children, and destroying the famous architectural monuments of one of the most beautiful cities in the world.

In the blockaded city there was a shortage of fuel, the city's transport system had been brought to a halt, the production of electricity was seriously curtailed, and the water supply had broken down. But it was famine which brought Leningrad nearest to disaster. The bread ration was cut to 125 grammes a day per person. Many thousands of people died an agonizing death. In these exceptionally trying conditions the defenders of Leningrad continued the fight and withstood the enemy.

In November the famous 'life-line' was laid across the ice-covered Ladoga lake. Under ceaseless bombardments and gun-fire, food and fuel began to reach Leningrad. And the city held out. Its defence was one of the most heroic episodes in the history of the Great Patriotic War.

The Atrocities Perpetrated by the Invaders

In those areas of our country which they temporarily occupied, the Hitlerites committed terrible crimes. The Fascist barbarians mercilessly exterminated Soviet citizens, party-members, trade unionists, collective farmers and Komsomol activists. People were shot if the enemy caught them breaking the most unimportant regulations. Concentration camps were created everywhere, and mass executions took place. Gallows stood at every corner.

The industrial enterprises which had been captured by the Hitlerites were declared the property of the Fascist Reich. The workers were forced to restore these enterprises. If anyone failed to turn up for work, they were beaten.

In the countryside the Hitlerites plundered and destroyed collective and state farms. German settlers began to appear in the Ukraine, in Byelorussia and in the Baltic States. The occupying forces took almost all the harvest away from the peasants. Millions of Soviet people were forcibly taken away to Fascist labour-camps in Germany. And yet Soviet citizens in the occupied areas did not bow to the invaders; they sabotaged in all possible ways their organization and commands, and helped wherever possible the partisans and the members of secret organizations.

Only a negligible number of the inhabitants of the occupied areas collaborated with the Hitlerites. In the main these people were the criminal element and the reactionary section of the clergy. The Soviet people treated the servants of the enemy with contempt. The partisans showed no mercy to the traitors.

Acting on the instructions of the Communist Party, the Soviet people formed partisan units behind the enemy lines. Communists and members of the Komsomol were the first to join the ranks of the partisans. Everywhere there grew up numerous groups dedicated to avenging the nation. This constituted a real threat to the invaders.

The Defeat of the German Fascist Troops outside Moscow

In a series of fierce battles, units of the Red Army halted the Fascists just outside Moscow. The Soviet High Command had brought up a significant number of reserves to the capital, deploying them in the main direction of the enemy offensive. Now it was the Soviet troops who had the advantage.

On 6 December, 1941, a tremendous artillery barrage marked the opening of the decisive counter-attack by troops of the Western Front, the Kalinin Front and the South-West Front under the command of General Zhukov, General Konev and Marshal Timoshenko. To the north of Moscow the Soviet troops shattered the enemy's resistance and, on the fifth day of the offensive, liberated Rogachev and surrounded Klin. To the south of Moscow our units inflicted a serious defeat on the German tank corps commanded by Guderian. In the course of fierce fighting, the enemy forces attempting to surround Moscow from the south were defeated and their scattered remnants withdrew southwards. On the central section of the front the Hitlerites were driven back from Kryukovo and Zvenigorod.

When they liberated the lands around Moscow, our troops saw the evidence of the dreadful crimes perpetrated by the Hitlerites. The Fascist butchers had shot, hanged, and tortured Soviet people in their thousands, and had killed even old men and children.

In the area around Moscow many towns had been destroyed and almost all the villages had been burnt. The Hitlerites had committed acts of vandalism against the great historic buildings of the Russian people. At Klin they had barbarously destroyed Tchaikovsky's house, near Tula they had plundered and set on fire Tolstoy's estate of Yasnaya Polyana. In the famous vaulted room where the great writer created his immortal novel *War and Peace*, the Hitlerites erected stalls for their horses. At Istra they had destroyed the 'New Jerusalem' church, the work of the great Russian architect Kazakov.

In the great battle for Moscow the Red Army brought to an end the legend of the invincibility of the Fascist army. The Hitler plan for a *blitzkrieg* had suffered a decisive rebuff. The defeat of the German Fascist forces outside the walls of the heroic city of Moscow was the most important event in the first year of the war and marked the first great defeat of the Hitlerites in the whole course of the Second World War.

CHAPTER VI

★

The War in the Pacific

★

Towards the end of 1941 the war spread to the Pacific Ocean. That summer Japan had occupied Indo-China (a French colony). She was making preparations for the seizure of Indonesia (a Dutch colony) and the possessions of the USA and England in the Pacific. At the same time the Japanese Government was carrying on negotiations with the Government of the USA to normalize Japanese-American relations. The only reason for these negotiations was to distract the USA's attention from the preparations being made by Japan to strike a sudden blow at American naval bases. The rulers of Japan knew that the imperialists of the United States counted on the Japanese armed forces attacking the USSR and were therefore not expecting an attack themselves. The Japanese militarists based their policy on the fact that it was easier to attack the American bases in the Pacific than start a war with the USSR. The military and political high command of Japan was planning first to seize the economic resources of the English, American and Dutch possessions in South-East Asia and the Pacific, and then to attack the USSR, which, according to their calculations, would by this time have been weakened by the war against Hitler's Germany.

On the morning of 7 December, 1941, the Japanese Air Force, based on aircraft-carriers, struck a sudden and concentrated blow at the most important naval base of the USA—Pearl Harbor in the Hawaiian islands. The United

States High Command had not built up the necessary defences to repel this blow by the aggressor. This caused the American Navy heavy losses. Out of eight battleships anchored in the harbour, four were sunk and four damaged, and eighteen warships were put out of action. Almost at the same time the Japanese sank several English warships in the South China Seas.

The position of the United States and England in the Pacific was weakened. The Japanese aggressors mounted a broad offensive in South-East Asia. By May, 1942, Japan had seized Malaya, Burma, the islands of Indonesia and of the Philippines. The Japanese troops took possession of the important English naval bases of Singapore and Hong Kong, occupied numerous islands in the Pacific which belonged to England and the United States, and invaded South-West China and Eastern India.

The Kuomintang Government of China,* which was to become ever more inclined to capitulate, was not waging active military operations against the Japanese invaders. The Chiang Kai-shek faction used the military aid it received from the United States not so much for fighting the Japanese invaders, as for exerting greater pressure on the regions controlled by the Communists. Allowing for the possibility of attacking Japan, the USSR throughout the whole war kept on her Far Eastern frontiers up to 40 divisions, a strong air force and fleet, thereby holding down the Japanese army and by this very fact supporting China.

In six months Japan had seized, with only insignificant losses on her part, a huge expanse of territory—3·8 million square kilometres—with a population of 150 million.

Following Japan's lead, Germany and Italy declared war on the United States. The war-zone became vastly broader. The USA's entry into the war strengthened the forces of the anti-Fascist coalition.

* The Chinese Nationalist Party led by Chiang Kai-shek.

CHAPTER VII

★

The Creation of the Anti-Fascist Coalition

✗

The victory outside Moscow finally brought about the decisive formation of an anti-Fascist coalition. On 1 January, 1942, in Washington, twenty-six states, including the USSR, the USA and England, signed the United Nations Declaration. They pledged themselves to make use of their resources for the struggle against the aggressors, to co-operate in waging the war and not to conclude a separate peace. Later, on 26 May, representatives of the Soviet Union and England met in London and signed an agreement of alliance in the war against Hitler's Germany and its accomplices in Europe. The agreement also provided for collaboration and mutual aid in the post-war world.

Simultaneously in Washington Soviet-American negotiations were set up, culminating in a written agreement on 11 June. Both sides pledged the mutual supply of defence materials and information, as well as the development of trade and economic collaboration.

The Governments of the USA and England, in entering into an anti-Fascist coalition, were pursuing their own imperialist aims. But the formation of the coalition was also a great success for Soviet foreign policy; it was the result of putting into practice the precepts of Lenin on how to take advantage of the deep conflict that exists between the imperialist states. The coalition came into being not only as a result of an agreement between the great powers, but its creation can also be attributed to the tremendous anti-Fascist struggle waged by millions, with the Communists always to the fore. Of great significance too was the pressure the mass of the people exerted on their Governments in England and the United States.

The mainspring and chief protagonist in the united anti-Fascist front of freedom-loving nations was the Soviet Union. The heaviest burden of the struggle against the Fascist hordes lay on the shoulders of the Soviet people and their armed forces.

The Difference in Aims between the Main Participants in the Coalition

Sharp differences of opinion existed between the members of the anti-Fascist coalition about the aims of the war, and about the programme of post-war reconstruction. The USSR was fighting for the defeat of Fascism, the liberation of the enslaved nations, the rebirth of democratic freedom and the creation of favourable conditions for the approaching peace.

The imperialists of the USA and England considered the main aim of the war to be the defeat of Germany and Japan in their capacity as chief rivals, and the consolidation of their domination of the world. At the same time reactionary circles in the USA and England were aiming to preserve Germany and Japan to provide military power for a struggle against the USSR.

The Soviet Union strictly observed the obligations placed upon her by this alliance, but the USA and England flagrantly infringed the conditions. In the course of Anglo-Soviet and Soviet-American negotiations, agreement was reached about the opening of the Second Front in Europe. In 1942 the USA and England had at their disposition a large body of armed forces and enormous military and technical reserves for waging war in Europe, and, what is more, 70 per cent of the German army was concentrated on the Eastern Front. However, the Western Powers deliberately deceived their ally. They preferred to await the course of events, expecting the exhaustion of the warring parties.

The delay in opening the Second Front postponed the defeat of Fascism and condemned to death yet more millions. For three years the Soviet Union waged a heroic struggle, practically on her own, against the Hitlerite hordes, thus saving world civilization from Fascist barbarism.

CHAPTER VIII

★

The North African Campaign

✶

The battle outside Moscow had caused the transfer of enemy troops from North Africa. In November, 1941, the English moved to the offensive and raised the blockade of Tobruk. Shortly afterwards the whole of Cyrenaica was freed. But the Fascists took advantage of the dispersion of English troops and in January, 1942, began an offensive in the course of which they again took possession of Cyrenaica. The Italian-German Air Force and Navy controlled the shipping lanes in the Mediterranean. The English had to withdraw to the Egyptian frontier. The advance of the Fascists towards the Suez Canal was halted on the defended frontier at El Alamein 100 kilometres west of Alexandria. The situation in North Africa was temporarily stabilized.

Because the main Fascist forces had been drawn on to the Soviet-German front, the English command, led by General Montgomery, could now build up their reserves and in October, 1942, begin an offensive. The enemy retreated from Egypt.

On 8 November, 1942, the Allies landed in force in French Morocco and Algeria, which were at that time under the control of the Vichy authorities, but these troops were slow in carrying out this offensive. During the whole of the military operations in North Africa, Germany did not move one division away from the Eastern Front.

By invading the French colonies, the USA and England

were acting in accord with their own imperialist interests. Each one of these powers counted on strengthening its own position there.

The defeat of the Hitlerites, who had flung the main body of their forces into the battle at Stalingrad, now created favourable conditions for an attack by Anglo-American troops in North Africa. In hot pursuit of the Fascists, the Allies occupied Cyrenaica and Tripolitania, followed by Tunis. In May, 1943, the Italian and German troops in North Africa surrendered utterly.

In June, 1943, the 'French Committee of National Liberation' was formed. In this the leading role was played by General de Gaulle.

The Allies Again Postpone Opening the Second Front

The United States and England, in the same way as before, delayed opening the Second Front. The chief opponent of an advance into Europe across the Channel was Churchill. He suggested making a landing in the Balkans, calling this area the 'soft under-belly of Europe'. Churchill's aim was to introduce allied troops into the countries of South-East Europe before the arrival of the Red Army, in order to install in these countries reactionary régimes dependent on England and the USA. The American leaders were afraid that the allied armies might get tied up in the Balkans, and they were more interested in establishing their influence in Western Europe. So Churchill's military and political plans were greeted with some reserve in Washington and in the end were not carried through.

In spite of repeated assurances by the Allies, the Second Front was not in fact opened in 1943. The Governments of the United States and England were well aware of the needs of the Red Army and of the tremendous losses sustained by the USSR in the war. But in the spring of 1943 they suspended the convoys of military supplies to the northern ports of the USSR and did not start them up again until eight months later. Delays such as this occurred repeatedly. The conduct of the Allies seriously impaired the trust placed in them by the USSR.

CHAPTER IX

★

Stalingrad

✗

The Fierce Defensive Battles in the Summer of 1942

Taking advantage of the absence of any Second Front in Europe, the Hitler command concentrated 237 divisions on the Soviet-German front in the summer of 1942, and by the autumn they had increased these to 266 divisions and were preparing a large-scale offensive. The enemy's aim was the destruction of the Soviet troops on the Western Don, and the capture of the extremely rich agricultural areas of the Don and the Kuban and the oil-fields of the Caucasus.

Following the capture of Stalingrad, they planned to cut our lines of communication along the Volga. The Hitlerites thought that a victory in this vital area would allow them to win a decisive campaign and bring the war to an end in 1942.

At the end of June the enemy, gathering its forces in a south-easterly direction, undertook a great offensive with forces outnumbering the Soviet troops two to one. Our units were hard-pressed by the German invaders, who succeeded in making a speedy advance towards the Volga in the direction of Stalingrad. At the same time the Fascist troops began to advance on the Caucasus and in several places moved forward towards the range of the Caucasus itself.

The Red Army was faced with the task of halting the enemy, come what may. 'Not one step backwards'—thus ran the command of the Fatherland. The commanding officers and political workers explained to the troops that to retreat further would be to court disaster, and that to withstand the enemy onslaught was to guarantee victory.

The Heroic Defence of Stalingrad

From the middle of July fierce battles against the superior forces of the enemy took place on the distant approaches to Stalingrad. This was the beginning of the mighty battle for Stalingrad. The Soviet troops just managed to hold off a furious attack by the enemy on the west bank of the Don. More than 150,000 inhabitants of Stalingrad, led by the regional party committee, built defensive lines. Workers increased the production of arms to fulfil the needs of the front. Every day forty tanks were sent straight from the factory conveyor belt to the front. Tens of thousands joined the People's Volunteer Corps and fighting battalions. In August the German-Fascist troops, who had the numerical advantage, forced a crossing over the River Don. At the cost of huge losses they succeeded in breaking through our front on 23 August and advancing towards the Volga. The enemy subjected the town to severe bombardment from the air. 'We have turned the town into a burning hell', boasted the Fascist airmen. German tanks broke through to the area around the tractor factory. But their attack was beaten off by the workers in the factory.

The Hitlerites continued to bring in fresh detachments and concentrated in this area more than a million soldiers, a fifth of all their infantry, and about a third of their tank divisions. Besides this, one Italian army and two Rumanian armies fought by their side. But all the time the enemy offensive was losing impetus. Only at the price of tremendously severe losses did the Hitlerites succeed on 13 September in getting really close to Stalingrad.

From that day on fierce fighting took place in the town itself, the defence of which was entrusted to the 62nd Army under the command of General Chuikov and the 64th Army commanded by General Shumilov.

The enemy tried to break our defences, isolate the defenders and annihilate them in groups. But all their attempts failed. From the left bank of the Volga our heavy artillery opened fire on the enemy every time they moved to the attack. Under the protection of this ceaseless artillery fire, which beat off the enemy air raids, ships of the Volga war flotilla floated across the river to the town military units. They ferried across thousands of tons of war materials, and evacuated the wounded to the left bank.

The Fascist command threw into the offensive thirty-six divisions, 2,000 aircraft and 1,500 guns. During the battle period the enemy air force made more than 70,000 flights and dropped more than a million bombs. The 13th Guards Division, under the command of General Rodimtsev, who were defending the centre of the town, had to withstand especially fierce attacks. The Soviet soldiers, with unshakeable valour, repulsed the enemy attacks and inflicted huge losses on them.

In October the Hitlerites managed in isolated places to break through to the Volga. The situation of the defenders of the town became critical, but their valour and bravery did not weaken. Among the ruins of impenetrable Stalingrad our valiant soldiers held out in battle against a strong and crafty foe. Because they had lost hundreds of thousands of men killed and wounded, and a large quantity of war materials, the Hitlerites were forced to cut short their attacks and pass to the defensive.

The Red Army's Triumphant Completion of the Battle of Stalingrad

From the end of 1942 the Great Patriotic War entered upon a new phase. The Red Army definitely passed to the attack, now that they had begun the massive expulsion of the

German-Fascist invaders from our soil. This attack started on the banks of the Volga. Even while the defensive battles raged, Soviet High Command, together with the commanding officers of the Stalingrad, Don and South-West fronts, had evolved a plan for a counter-offensive, which was to lead to the surrounding and defeat of all the enemy forces in the Stalingrad area.

To the north-west of Stalingrad, unknown to the enemy, large forces of Soviet infantry, tanks, artillery, aircraft and other troops were concentrated. Now that we had equality with the enemy in the number of our troops, and a certain advantage in artillery and tanks, the Soviet Command could deploy significantly superior forces to deliver severe blows to the enemy.

In the period prior to the counter-attack close attention was paid to the military and political preparation of officers and men. Newspapers distributed at the front, military leaflets, exhortation by word of mouth—all these means were brought into play in order to inspire the Soviet soldiers with an exalted enthusiasm for the attack and determination and resolve in the forthcoming operations.

One foggy morning, 19 November, 1942, a great force of Soviet artillery rumbled along the banks of the Don and the Volga, hundreds of planes bearing the Red Star soared into the air. A heavy artillery bombardment lasting eighty minutes preceded the attack, then the troops of the South-Western and Don fronts, commanded by General Vatutin and General Rokossovsky, moved to the offensive.

Shock units of tanks battered the enemy defences. Caught unawares, the enemy troops wavered and began to fall back. The following day, 20 November, the troops of the Stalingrad front, under the command of General Yeremenko, joined the attack and broke through the enemy defences. Mechanized divisions drove through the breach that had been made in the enemy lines. As a result of this speedy attack the troops of the Stalingrad front joined up with those of the South-Western front on 22 November in the area around the town of Kalach. Thus they surrounded twenty-two German Fascist divisions, numbering 330,000 men, together with a large quantity of military equipment.

The Hitler command made a desperate attempt to break through the ring of encircling troops and to rescue their own forces. On 12 December a powerful motorized company of Fascist troops, commanded by Field-Marshal Manstein, launched an offensive from the direction of Kotelnikovo. 'Be assured of our aid', Manstein radioed boastfully to his surrounded troops.

In these battles a member of the Komsomol, Ilya Kaplunov, who was serving in the Volga defence forces, gave an example of unparalleled heroism. While his company was engaged in repelling an enemy attack, though isolated and surrounded, he attacked a whole group of tanks and, with accurate fire from his anti-tank rifle, he put three Fascist machines out of action. When his ammunition ran out, Kaplunov seized some anti-tank grenades and crawled out of his shelter. He succeeded in blowing up another two tanks. But at that moment this heroic Komsomol member was mortally wounded by shell-splinters. Gathering his last remnants of strength, he continued to crawl forward, leaving a trail of blood in the snow. One after another, his grenades set on fire another four Fascist tanks. When the battle subsided, Kaplunov's friends sought him out. He was dead. Around him were nine Fascist tanks, blown up and blazing. Kaplunov, who had kept on smashing the enemy right up to his last breath, received the posthumous award of 'Hero of the Soviet Union'.

In order that Manstein should be defeated as quickly as possible, the Stalingrad front was strengthened by bringing up the 2nd Guards Army, commanded by General Malinovsky. The enemy division at Kotelnikovo was smashed by a counter-blow from our forces. The surrounded Hitler troops found themselves in a hopeless position. The front moved 300 kilometres further west.

On 8 January the Soviet command delivered an ultimatum calling for the capitulation of the surrounded German Fascist troops. But Hitler ordered them to continue their resistance, and the ultimatum was declined. Then the Soviet troops began military operations to exterminate this company of enemy soldiers, and on 2 February, 1943, it ceased to exist. The bodies of 147,200 Fascist officers and men who had been killed in the fight were picked up from the battlefield and buried. The Soviet troops took prisoner 91,000, including 2,500 officers and twenty-four generals, together with General-Fieldmarshal Paulus.

A Letter Home from Reuben Ibarruri* on the Eastern Front:

'I am taking advantage of a spare moment to write these few lines. You mustn't worry about me, as I am getting on O.K.

'Mama, when I said goodbye to you you told me not to be afraid. I thought that was almost an insult, and I must tell you that my hands won't tremble when I kill those dogs.

'Once again, Mama, I must tell you that I consider it an honour and a source of pride that I have the chance to fight in the ranks of the great and invincible Red Army against the tyrant of humankind. I am sure that here he will smash his teeth in, for, as I told you, here in every woman and in every man there lives a hero, a bolshevik. These people are really amazing. I can tell you that sometimes I am moved to the depths of my soul. Such people just cannot be beaten.

'That's all for today. Much love from your loving son,

*Reuben Ibarruri was the son of the Spanish Communist leader, Dolores Ibarruri.

whose wish is that you should keep on working harder and harder for the sake of our cause.'

The International Significance of the Victory at Stalingrad

The battle at Stalingrad was the greatest military and political event of the Second World War. This victory turned out to be the beginning of a fundamental change in the course of the war to the advantage of the USSR and the whole of the anti-Fascist coalition. From the banks of the Volga the Red Army began its advance which culminated in the unconditional surrender of Hitler's Germany.

The scale of the German defeat at Stalingrad, unprecedented in the history of war, made the ruling circles of Japan regard matters in a more sober light and staved off Japan's entry into the war against the USSR. It also upset the calculations of Turkey's rulers, who although formally neutral, were in fact assisting Germany and were waiting for the fall of Stalingrad to enter the war on the side of Germany.

★

CHAPTER X

The Resistance Movements in the Occupied Countries

✶

The victory at Stalingrad inspired a surge of new activity in the resistance movement. As this movement grew two distinct political lines emerged.

The bourgeois émigré governments and their supporters were not wholeheartedly fighting Fascism; they wished to keep the liberation of their countries under their control. They feared that if the mass of the people joined the struggle to get rid of the invaders, a popular government would replace their bourgeois one after liberation. So, for example, the Polish émigré Government forbade the army divisions under its control to fight the occupying forces. They were ordered to wait 'with weapons at their sides' until 'the two enemies fighting each other' should achieve mutual annihilation.

The other line of policy, pursued by the Communist parties, strove to create a united national front against Fascism and reaction.

In France, the National Resistance Council was created on the initiative of the Communists. More and more patriots, escaping deportation to Germany, disappeared into the woods to fight the occupying forces. Many of them died a hero's death. The guerrilla groups blew up bridges, derailed troop trains and killed the Fascist butchers. In the port of Toulon the sailors scuttled the national fleet to prevent it being handed over to Hitler's troops. The French Communist party, which had the popular name of the 'party of the executed', lost 75,000 of its members in its fight with the invaders.

Great valour and heroism in fighting the enemy was shown by the Communists of Czechoslovakia. Twenty-five thousand members of the party died at the hands of the Hitlerites. Among them was the fearless son of the Czech people, Julius Fuchik. In prison he wrote his moving book—*Report Written with a Noose round my Neck*. It concludes with a passionate appeal addressed to the living: 'People, I loved you. Be vigilant'.

An armed struggle against the Fascist invaders was carried on without cease on Yugoslav and Albanian soil. In Yugoslavia, the guerrilla divisions grew into the National Liberation Army, whose numbers reached 300,000 by the end of 1943. In Poland in 1942 there emerged the 'People's Guard'. This was the name of a body of guerrillas organized by the Communists, which engaged in a determined struggle against the occupying forces. The 'People's Guard' formed the basis of the People's Army, created in 1944.

The anti-Fascist movement was also growing in the countries which belonged to the Hitler bloc. Underground groups led by the Communists were active in Berlin, Hamburg, Munich and other large German towns. Real patriotism was shown by those Germans who sought out important information in order to help the USSR to defeat Fascism. They distributed illegal newspapers and leaflets which exposed the evils of Hitlerism, planned escapes from prisons and concentration camps, and organized acts of sabotage in factories.

Many Soviet people among those driven by the Hitlerites into slavery and those who had escaped from German prisoner-of-war camps behaved, outside the borders of their native land, like true patriotic warriors. Soviet citizens bravely fought in the guerrilla movements of the occupied countries of Europe, thus making their contribution to the common cause of victory over Fascist Germany.

Everywhere in the course of the struggle against the Hitlerites and local traitors, the unity of anti-Fascist forces became more marked and National Fronts were set up. The Communists headed national democratic bodies which became the basis of national authority. The struggle for liberation waged by the peoples of Europe against Hitlerism, inflicted severe losses on the invaders, weakened the Fascist rear and brought nearer the victory over the hated enemy.

The Disbanding of the Comintern and its Historical Significance

The Communist parties honourably withstood the severe trials that fell to their share. The influence and authority of the Communists over the mass of the people showed a significant growth. New warriors came forward into the line to replace the fallen. The world Communist movement grew stronger and became tempered in the fight. On the eve of the war the Communist parties had a membership of 4·2 million; at the end of the war their members already numbered 20 million.

The various Marxist-Leninist parties abroad had accumulated experience in the class struggle, had personnel well tried and tempered, and could assume independent leadership of the masses. The complicated conditions surrounding the revolutionary struggle in the war years demanded of the Communist parties that they should be extremely flexible and willing to manœuvre. It became impossible to lead them from one international centre. Therefore in May, 1943, the Praesidium of the Political Committee of the Comintern passed a resolution dissolving the Communist International. All the Communist parties approved this decision. It decisively gave the lie to the bourgeois calumny that the

Communist parties acted only on orders from the Comintern and did not serve the interests of their own nations. The disbanding of the Comintern, which in no way signified a weakening of proletarian solidarity, facilitated the uniting of all progressive forces in every country into a single anti-Fascist front and helped to strengthen the anti-Hitler coalition.

The Communist International had fulfilled its historical mission. It had trained and tempered the Communist parties, had prepared them for solving independently the complicated problems facing the working class. The Comintern had preserved Marxism-Leninism from being distorted by opportunists; it had worked out in new conditions theoretical and tactical questions concerning the working-class movement, and had produced experienced and steadfast party-leaders.

CHAPTER XI

★

Soviet Victories in 1943

✶

After the battle of Stalingrad, the German forces in the northern Caucasus faced a serious threat of encirclement. So in January, 1943, they began a hasty retreat and soon the northern Caucasus was completely free of the invader.

Also in January, 1943, units of the Red Army in a counter-offensive to the south of Lake Ladoga broke the blockade of Leningrad, forging a corridor between eight and nine kilometres wide. As early as the beginning of February a railway was constructed linking the citizens of Leningrad with the rest of the country. Train-loads of food and fuel managed to get through to Leningrad despite a constant hail of enemy fire.

In January and February the Soviet forces launched a successful offensive against Kursk, Kharkov and the Basin of the Don, driving the invader out of Voronezh, Kursk, and then Rzhev, Gzhatsk* and Vyazma. As a result of the winter offensive of 1942-3 the Red Army advanced 600-700 kilometres westwards along a 1,500-kilometre front which stretched from the northern Caucasus to Leningrad.

From July, 1942, to February, 1943, the Hitlerites had lost about one and a half million men killed and wounded.

The Defeat of the Enemy Forces at Kursk

After their serious reverses in the winter of 1942-3 the

* Now Gagarin.

Fascist command decided to take their revenge in a summer offensive. Germany had introduced universal conscription (which enabled about two million more men to be called to the colours), and also transferred new troops from Western Europe. The German command was therefore able to position 257 divisions along the Soviet-German front by the summer of 1943.

Out of this number, the Hitlerites concentrated in the Kursk area an army of nearly a million men, together with tens of thousands of weapons, aircraft and tanks. In this region, as a result of the Red Army spring offensive, a salient had been formed (the Kursk bulge) which projected into the enemy lines. The Fascist command decided to launch an offensive from the springboards of Orel and Belgorod, with the intention of surrounding our troops and continuing the attack in a north-easterly direction. The Hitlerites pinned their hopes on the surprise element of the new large 'Tiger' and 'Panther' tanks, and the self-propelling 'Ferdinand' guns, which were to be used for the first time on a large scale.

But the Soviet command, who had discovered the enemy's intentions, had already carefully planned both the defence of the area and a counter-attack by our troops. In the area of the 'Kursk bulge' there were important concentrations of our reserve troops and strong defence fortifications.

Military intelligence had succeeded in finding out the day and even the hour of the enemy attack. At dawn on 5 July, just when the Hitlerites intended to begin to attack, the Soviet artillery opened up a terrific barrage of fire, which inflicted heavy losses on the enemy. However, the German Fascist offensive was launched as planned. From the Orel region more than 500 German tanks moved forward against the Soviet troop positions, and another 1,000 or more from the Belgorod region. In their wake came the infantry. The enemy troops had massive air support. But the enemy plan failed. Their furious land and air attacks were smashed on encountering the boundless resolve of the Soviet soldiers. Our glorious men of the tank corps, artillery and infantry again afforded examples of devoted heroism. One of our regiments was pounded by two thousand separate attacks from the air, followed by an advance by 150 tanks. The Fascist armour tried sixteen times to break through the regiment's defences but the Soviet soldiers retreated not one step.

The Soviet troops not only held the enemy's attack, but even counter-attacked themselves. A particularly massive counter-blow was aimed at the enemy on 12 July in the Prokhorovka region. On this day a tank battle took place which was unprecedented in its scale. Altogether 1,500 tanks took part in this battle, plus hundreds of self-propelled weapons and a large number of aircraft. On this day alone the enemy lost more than 400 tanks.

In seven days of intense fighting the enemy did not succeed in breaking through the Soviet defences on any section of the front. As a result of their huge losses in men and materials the German Fascist troops managed to advance only nine to fifteen kilometres in the Orel–Kursk direction, and only fifteen to thirty-five kilometres in the Belgorod–Kursk direction. Their summer offensive had failed.

The Red Army Counter-Offensive

With the enemy now exhausted and drained of their strength, all the units of the Red Army passed to the offensive. On 5 August, after stubborn fighting, the towns of Orel and Belgorod were liberated. On that day an artillery salute was fired for the first time in Moscow in honour of a victory of the Soviet troops. In the distant past it had been a tradition for a victory gained by our troops to be marked by an artillery salute in the capital.

Taking advantage of the success they had gained in the

direction of Belgorod, the Soviet troops began an attack on Kharkov. The Hitlerites' desperate attempts to hold the town had no success. On 23 August Kharkov was liberated.

The Battle for the Dnieper: The Liberation of Kiev

The victory in the battle of Kursk marked the end of the great summer and autumn offensive of the Red Army on a vast front 2,000 kilometres long—from Velikiye-Luki to the Taman Peninsula. In the space of two months our forces had freed the Don Basin, the Taman Peninsula, almost all the left-bank Ukraine, and the towns of Bryansk and Smolensk. By the end of September the Red Army had advanced to the Dnieper on a front 700 kilometres wide.

The Soviet troops, with unparalleled bravery, forced the Dnieper simultaneously at Gomel, Kiev, Kremenchug and Dnepropetrovsk. For the heroism they displayed in this operation, 2,000 or so of our troops, generals, officers, non-commissioned officers and men were honoured with the lofty title of Hero of the Soviet Union. Many thousands of Soviet soldiers were awarded ribbons and medals.

At the beginning of November, 1943, an attack was launched in the direction of Kiev. Here the troops of the 1st Ukraine front, under the command of General Vatutin, carried out a skirting manœuvre and, on 6 November, after intense fighting, liberated Kiev, the capital of the Soviet Ukraine.

The Hitlerites launched furious counter-attacks. Stubborn fighting went on for a whole month to the west of Kiev, and as a result the Soviet troops pushed the Fascists further west.

Thus, the offensive during the summer and autumn of 1943, had brought the Red Army a resounding victory. The Soviet troops had freed almost two-thirds of the land which had been occupied by the enemy; they had rescued from Fascist bondage many millions of Soviet citizens, and they

1. Enlisting for the Great Patriotic War, 1941.

2. "Become experts at your jobs"—signalmen in training.

3. A partisan detachment in the Smolensk area.

4. Red army orderlies crawl under fire towards
their wounded comrades.

5. Five Eastern Front partisans about to be hanged.

6. Stalingrad, 1943—Russian troops celebrate the defeat of the German forces.

7. Stalingrad.

8. A sixty-four-year-old Cossack volunteer.

9. Zoya Kosmodemyanskaya, partisan heroine, on her way to her execution.

10. Luftwaffe troops flush out a shelter in Russia 1942.

The editor and publishers are grateful to the Robert Hunt
Library for permission to reproduce copyright illustrations.

had restored to their Fatherland some most important industrial and agricultural regions. One hundred and eighteen enemy divisions had been defeated—half of the complete strength of the enemy forces on the Soviet-German front. Now the Red Army had gained rich experience in warfare and was superior to the enemy, not only in quality but also in quantity of armaments.

The successful summer and autumn offensive of the Red Army brought about a radical change in the nature and purpose of military operations. The initiative had definitely passed into the hands of the Soviet Armed Forces. Thus did 1943 go down in history as the year of radical change in the course of the Great Patriotic War and in the course of the whole of the Second World War.

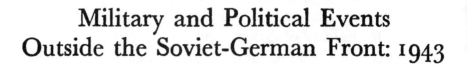

CHAPTER XII

Military and Political Events
Outside the Soviet-German Front: 1943

After the defeat of the Hitler troops at Stalingrad and in the later campaigns of 1943, almost two-thirds of the Soviet soil temporarily occupied by the Fascists had been liberated. The shattering blows delivered by the Soviet troops, especially the great defeat suffered by the German Fascist army in the summer of 1943 in the Battle of Kursk, rendered inevitable the complete collapse of Hitler's Germany.

The Capitulation of Italy

The defeats suffered by the Hitlerites and their allies shook the rear of the Fascist bloc. Italy had lost eleven divisions in battles with the Red Army. It had also suffered serious losses in North Africa. The economy of the country was disrupted. The Germans had transformed Italy into a base for the supplies of goods and raw materials to Germany. The Italian workers, under the leadership of the Communists, waged a steadfast fight against the Fascist régime and the wave of strikes which had hit the industrial areas of the country in the spring of 1943 hastened the break-up of Italian Fascism.

In July, 1943, Anglo-American troops seized the island of Sicily. In Italy a political crisis quickly came to a head. The ruling circles of Italy wished to preserve the system of exploitation. Relying on the support of the top bourgeoisie and the military 'brass-hats', the King dismissed Mussolini from his post of head of the government. Marshal Badoglio formed a new government. The masses of the people demanded an immediate peace and the overthrow of Fascism. The Government entered into negotiations with the allies and capitulated.

In September, 1943, the Anglo-American troops landed in the south of Italy. At that time the Hitlerites occupied the northern and central provinces of the country, as well as part of the south. The surrender of Italy—the chief ally of Germany in Europe—laid the foundations for the downfall of the Fascist bloc.

Following the orders of Hitler, the SS Officer Otto Skorzeny flew in with a parachute division and freed Mussolini, who was then in prison. Soon the Duce was heading the puppet government of the 'Italian Socialist Republic', set up on territory occupied by the German Fascist troops.

The Italian workers rose in armed combat against the Fascists. After the capitulation the Italian people began a war of liberation against the Hitlerite invaders and local Fascists. The Committees of National Liberation led the struggle. The Resistance movement combined into one group all the anti-Fascist forces—Communists, socialists, Catholics and others. The Communist Party created 'Garibaldi brigades' which formed the nucleus of the partisan army and 'Corps of Freedom Volunteers'. At the time of the most extensive operations it united more than a thousand partisan divisions. In the liberated zones democratic procedures were being established.

The Teheran Conference

From 28 November to 1 December, 1943, in Teheran, the capital of Iran, the heads of government of the three allied powers—J. V. Stalin, F. Roosevelt and W. Churchill—met in conference. In spite of Churchill's opposition, the conference took the decision to open the Second Front in Western Europe in May, 1944. It was clear that the USSR was now capable of defeating Germany with its own forces, thus freeing the whole of Europe from Fascist tyranny. The declaration made at the conference dealt with joint operations in the war against Germany, and also with post-war co-operation. The decisions of the conference strengthened the anti-Fascist coalition and instilled into the consciousness of the peoples a firm assurance of victory over the common enemy.

But the reactionary circles of the USA and England continued to nurture anti-Soviet plans. They were relying on the preservation of the bourgeois landowner structure in Poland, Rumania and Hungary and on the creation of a *cordon sanitaire* along the western frontiers of the USSR. Unknown to the Soviet Government, representatives of the USA and England secretly carried on negotiations with confidential agents of Hitler for a separate peace. By doing this the Western powers badly betrayed their obligations as allies.

CHAPTER XIII

★

The Year of Decisive Victories

✶

The Military Situation at the Beginning of 1944

In the new year of 1944 the Soviet Armed Forces were stronger than ever before. Now they had an extensive experience of action in the field and were well supplied with modern military equipment. The Red Army was thirteen times superior to the enemy in the number of troops, seventeen times stronger in the number of weapons and multi-rail rocket projectors, 1·4 times stronger in tanks and 2·7 times in aircraft.

The Great Patriotic War entered its final stage. The order of the day now was to drive the German Fascist invaders beyond the frontiers of the Soviet lands, and thereafter to eliminate the Fascist 'New Order' in Western Europe.

But the enemy was still powerful. Out of the 376 divisions belonging to Fascist Germany and her vassals at the end of 1943, 257 were fighting against Soviet troops. German industry and the factories of the occupied countries were turning out more military equipment than ever before for the Fascist troops.

The Red Army was faced with the task of dealing mighty blows at the enemy on different sections of the front and thus sweeping the Fascist invaders quickly from Soviet soil.

The Defeat of the German Troops at Leningrad, in Eastern Ukraine and in the Crimea

On 14 January, 1944, the troops on the Leningrad and

Volkhov fronts, supported by the Baltic fleet, passed to the attack at Leningrad and Novgorod. In two weeks of offensive battles they defeated the 18th German Army and drove the enemy troops back to a position sixty to ninety kilometres from Leningrad. Lenin's great city was finally freed from the enemy blockade.

At the end of February Soviet troops drove the invaders from the Leningrad and Novgorod areas and set foot on the soil of Soviet Estonia. The troops of the 1st and 2nd Ukrainian fronts, commanded by General Vatutin and General Konev, had begun offensive operations in Eastern Ukraine, and at the end of January and beginning of February they surrounded ten German divisions in the Korsun-Shevchenkovskiy region and defeated them.

In spite of the extremely muddy conditions owing to the bad weather, the troops of these fronts continued the offensive and in March, 1944, they crossed the frontier between the USSR and Rumania. At the same time troops of the 3rd and 4th Ukrainian fronts, commanded by General Malinovsky and General Tolbukhin, defeated the German troops in the Southern Ukraine and liberated the towns of Nikolayev and Odessa. As a result of these operations the large enemy forces in Eastern Ukraine were defeated. The Soviet troops did not allow the enemy time to come to their senses, but forced a passage over the River Prut and entered Rumania.

In April, 1944, the troops of the 4th Ukrainian front almost completely liberated the Crimea. The Germans tried to hold Sevastopol, but on 7 May our troops began to storm the town and by the evening of 9 May they were in possession of Sevastopol. The remnants of the Fascist troops who tried to flee by boat were drowned.

As a result of the winter and spring offensive of 1944, the Red Army had cleared the enemy from more than three-quarters of the Soviet territory they had occupied, had reached the state frontiers of the USSR along more than 400 kilometres of its length, and was now in a position to lend immediate aid to the peoples of South-Eastern Europe in their struggle against the German Fascist barbarians.

As our troops were now crossing the State boundary the Soviet Government again declared that the Red Army's aim was to free the peoples of Europe from Fascist slavery, to help them to re-create their own independent national states and to decide freely the question of their social and political organization.

The Opening of the Second Front

In June, 1944, when it had become obvious that the Soviet Union was capable of defeating Hitler's Germany with her forces alone, England and the USA opened the Second Front.

On 6 June the Allied forces, commanded by General Eisenhower, landed in Normandy (Northern France). The Anglo-American forces met with practically no opposition from the Hitlerites, and advanced into the heart of France. At the call of the French Communist party, an armed rising began in Paris on 19 August. The Fascist garrison was defeated. In a few days the Allied forces entered Paris which had been freed by the patriots.

Massive national risings also broke out in other regions of the country. Many *départements* rid themselves of the Hitlerite occupying troops before the arrival of the American and English troops. The Resistance fighters freed large towns such as Bordeaux and Marseilles. Towards the end of 1944 the territory of France was entirely freed of the Fascist invaders.

For these operations the Germans had diverted only sixty divisions to the Western front, while the Hitler command maintained 259 divisions and brigades on the Soviet-German front. The Soviet-German front remained the most important front and the most decisive one in the Second World War.

The Liberation of Karelia and Byelorussia

In June the troops of the Leningrad and Karelian fronts passed to the attack on the Karelian isthmus and in Karelia itself. They liberated a large part of Karelia and reached the frontier between the USSR and Finland. On 4 September, 1944, Finland surrendered unconditionally.

From 23 June to 29 August one of the most important operations in Byelorussia was carried on by the troops of the three Byelorussia fronts and the 1st Baltic front.

On 23 June Soviet troops launched an offensive on a broad front—from the Western Dvina to the River Pripet. They broke through the enemy's lines and a few days later surrounded and annihilated large enemy concentrations in the region around Bobruysk and Vitebsk.

Prior to the offensive launched by our troops, partisans had disrupted rail communications behind the enemy lines. Acting in collaboration with the attacking troops of the Red Army, the partisans took part in the annihilation of the surrounded enemy concentrations.

Now that they had defeated the flanks of the enemy troop concentrations, the troops of the 1st and 3rd Byelorussian fronts launched an offensive against Minsk and on 3 July, 1944, they freed the capital of Soviet Byelorussia.

Continuing the offensive, the Red Army had, by the end of August, completely liberated the Byelorussia Soviet Socialist Republic, part of Poland, which was one of our allies, a large part of Soviet Lithuania and had come near to the frontiers of East Prussia. The Soviet troops had advanced more than 500 kilometres towards the west, and had besides utterly routed the enemy troops in the central section of the front, annihilating or taking prisoner 540,000 enemy officers and men.

The Situation in Poland

The Polish people, who had groaned for five years under the Fascist yoke, joyfully greeted their liberators—the Soviet troops who had set foot upon their soil. The Polish patriots set up a Polish National Liberation Committee.

The forces of internal reaction, in order to prevent the patriotic National Liberation Committee from being established, decided to mount an uprising in Warsaw, to seize the capital before it was entered by Soviet troops, and to put the émigré government into power. Many inhabitants of Warsaw took part in the uprising, which began on 1 August, 1944. The Soviet command was not given advance notice of the uprising, which took place with little or no preparation. There were insufficient arms and ammunition. The attempt of the Soviet troops to link up with the insurgents was not crowned with success. By the beginning of October the Hitler troops had put down the rising and razed Warsaw to its foundations.

Not far from Lublin Soviet troops discovered evidence of one of the most dreadful Fascist crimes. The Hitler butchers had transported here, to the death camp of Maidanek, millions of people from all over Europe. They were brutally tortured and humiliated and then driven into the gas-chambers and put to death with 'cyclone' gas. For days on end smoke rose from the chimneys of the crematoriums in which the Fascists were burning the people. A million and a half Russians, Poles, Czechs, Jews, Frenchmen and Dutchmen were killed at Maidanek by the Fascist butchers. More than four million were exterminated in the other death camp—Oswiecim [Auschwitz]. The Red Army destroyed the Hitlerite death camps.

The Liberation of the Western Ukraine and Moldavia

In July the troops of the 1st Ukrainian front launched an offensive in the Western Ukraine. As a result of five days of intense fighting, they broke through the enemy defences and began to advance. On 27 July Lvov was liberated, and the whole of the Western Ukraine was freed by the end of August. Our troops forced a passage over the River Vistula and in a series of stubborn battles they established a springboard on its western bank.

On 20 August the troops of the 2nd and 3rd Ukrainian fronts opened an offensive in Moldavia. On 25 August tank corps and mechanized units from the two fronts surrounded twenty-two Fascist divisions in the area around Kishinev and Iasi, and in a few days' time these divisions were finally defeated.

The Attempted Assassination of Hitler

The heavy defeats suffered by the German Fascist army marked a sharp deterioration in the situation of Germany. The crisis in the Fascist régime grew ever more serious. A group of generals and financial magnates organized a plot against Hitler. The conspirators wished to eliminate the Führer, to conclude a separate peace with England and the USA and with them to agree about combined action against the USSR. However, the attempt to assassinate Hitler, undertaken on 20 July, 1944, ended in failure. The bomb left by one of the conspirators in Hitler's GHQ exploded, but Hitler remained alive. The members of the conspiracy were thrown into confusion. Soon they were captured and executed.

The Fascists took advantage of the attempt on Hitler's life to intensify even further the reign of terror in their own country. In August, 1944, the Hitlerites killed in villainous fashion the leader of the German Communists, Ernst Thälmann.

The Liberation of the Peoples of South-Eastern Europe

During this period the Rumanian patriotic forces, led by the Communist party, launched an armed rising against the Fascist clique of Antonescu. On 23 August, 1944, the Fascist dictatorship was overthrown. The new Rumanian Government declared war on Germany.

On 31 August the Red Army, joyfully greeted by the population, entered Bucharest. During September, the Soviet troops drove the Fascist invaders completely from Rumanian soil. Right up to the time when the Red Army reached the frontier between Rumania and Bulgaria, the monarchical-Fascist Government of Bulgaria continued to help Hitler's Germany. The Soviet Government could not consider these actions as anything other than the virtual participation of Bulgaria in the war on the side of Germany. On 5 September, 1944, the Soviet Government declared that 'not only was Bulgaria in a state of war with the USSR, but the Soviet Union too was henceforth in a state of war with Bulgaria'. The Red Army entered Bulgarian territory. On 9 September the workers of Bulgaria, led by their Communist party with Dimitrov at its head, staged an armed rising and overthrew the monarchical-Fascist dictatorship. A government of the Patriotic front came to power and declared war on Germany.

Military Successes on the Northern Front

In mid-September the troops of the three Baltic and Leningrad fronts passed to the offensive in the Baltic.

The troops of the Leningrad front broke the enemy's stubborn resistance, and on 22 September they liberated Tallinn, the capital of the Estonian SSR. The enemy offered especially fierce resistance around Riga. On 13 October, after months of intense fighting, Riga, the capital of Soviet Latvia, was liberated. At the same time units of the 1st Baltic front battled their way towards the Baltic coast and in the Liepaja region they cut off thirty German divisions. As a result of the Baltic operations the Estonian SSR and a large part of the Latvian SSR were completely liberated.

At the same time troops of the Karelian front, in collaboration with the Northern fleet, broke through the mighty defences of the enemy in Zanolyar and proceeded through Northern Finland to Norway, thus laying the foundations for the future liberation of that country.

The Red Army Offensive in Czechoslovakia, Hungary and Yugoslavia

In October the troops of the 2nd, 3rd and 4th Ukrainian fronts passed to the attack. A Czech corps, the Yugoslav National Liberation Army, and Bulgarian and Rumanian troops took part together with our troops in these battles against the Hitlerites. Covering the road into Southern Germany, the Fascist command concentrated more than eighty divisions in Hungary and Yugoslavia. But the Soviet troops were superior to the enemy in tanks, artillery and aircraft. The enemy put up a furious resistance and launched a series of counter-attacks. The fighting around Budapest was especially fierce.

Attacking in the difficult conditions of mountain terrain, troops of the 4th Ukrainian front had liberated all of the Ukraine beyond the Carpathians and had entered Czechoslovakia by the end of October, thus beginning its liberation from the Fascist oppressors.

At the end of September troops of the 3rd Ukrainian front passed to the attack in Yugoslavia. On 20 October, together with the Yugoslav National Liberation Army, they freed Belgrade. While this was going on, troops of the 2nd and 3rd

Ukrainian fronts launched an attack on Budapest, and on 26 December they completely surrounded the enemy troops there, numbering 160,000.

On 21 December the democratic forces of Hungary had set up a temporary national government which broke with Fascist Germany and declared war on it.

The enemy made desperate attempts to help their units surrounded in Budapest. But all these attempts ended in disaster. Eventually, on 16 February, after six weeks of furious fighting, our troops took Budapest and exterminated the enemy troops.

The Heroism of Soviet Captives

Those Soviet citizens who had been forcibly sent into hard labour in Germany or had been taken prisoner, keeping faith with their Fatherland, continued the struggle against the enemy. They formed underground cells in concentration camps, communicated the true position at the front line to fellow prisoners and organized escapes. Soviet citizens working in industrial enterprises in Nazi territory carried out effective sabotage.

A high example of patriotism was given by the Soviet General Karbishev. During a battle he was wounded and taken prisoner by the Hitlerites. For three and a half years they tortured him, suggesting that he should betray his Fatherland and go over to their side. Karbishev indignantly refused these proposals and waged an active underground struggle. In February, 1945, Karbishev was brutally put to death by the Hitlerites.

Thousands of Soviet patriots who had escaped from the Fascist torture chambers fought heroically in the partisan detachments in Poland, Czechoslovakia, Yugoslavia, France and Italy. In the summer of 1944, 17 per cent of all the Czech partisans (more than 2,000 soldiers) was made up of Soviet citizens. In Yugoslavia, a whole partisan brigade was composed exclusively of Soviet escapees from Hitlerite camps.

The Results of the Military Operations in 1944

In the course of 1944 the Red Army had fought their way forward and advanced 500 to 1,000 kilometres, and had defeated large concentrations of enemy troops. As a result of these successful operations, a number of most important problems were solved.

Firstly, all the Soviet territory which had been temporarily occupied was now freed, and the state frontier of the USSR was completely restored from the Barents Sea to the Black Sea.

Secondly, the Red Army had smashed all the enemy armed forces which had been on the territory of the USSR, Rumania, Yugoslavia, Hungary and Finland.

Thirdly, the whole of the Hitler bloc, that marauding gang of robbers, had been split apart and routed. Italy first ceased to be Germany's ally, and in 1944 Finland, Rumania, Bulgaria, and Hungary followed suit. These countries declared war on Germany and made their contribution to the final defeat of Fascism. Even those states which had occupied a position of benevolent neutrality vis-à-vis Germany (Turkey, Chile, Argentina and others), now formally declared war on her.

Fourthly, the Red Army had brought the peoples of Eastern and South-Eastern Europe freedom from the Fascist yoke. The defeat of the German Fascist troops on the territory of Rumania, Bulgaria and Hungary facilitated the overthrow of the reactionary pro-Fascist régimes by the peoples of these countries, who could then create democratic governments and embark upon the path of national democratic reforms. The basis was laid for the liberation of

Czechoslovakia and Poland, a large part of Yugoslavia was freed and Norway had begun to be liberated.

Now the Soviet land and her valiant armed forces were ready to deal the final blow at the enemy.

CHAPTER XIV

★

The Final Defeat of Fascist Germany

✶

The Crimean Conference

In the situation brought about by the great new victories won by the Red Army, there took place in the Crimea (at Yalta), from 4 to 11 February, 1945, a conference of the heads of government of the USSR, the USA and England. A plan of campaign was worked out for the decisive defeat of Germany and the basic principles for post-war reconstruction were established. The heads of the three governments declared that the aim of the Allied Powers was the annihilation of German militarism and Fascism, and also the creation of guarantees that Germany would never again be able to destroy the world. The Allies pledged themselves to carry out a co-ordinated policy in those countries freed from Fascist tyranny, to promote the renewal of their independence, to aid their democratic development, and to provide these countries with economic assistance.

However, not long before the end of the war in Europe, in direct contradiction to the obligations he had undertaken, Churchill ordered the English military command to collect together German arms, so that 'if the inevitable need arose they could be again distributed to German soldiers and used against the USSR'.

At the Crimea Conference a secret agreement was reached concerning the USSR's entry into the war against Japan in two to three months after the capitulation of Germany at the end of the war in Europe.

The Soviet Forces' Offensive in the Winter of 1945

At the beginning of 1945 the Soviet Armed Forces had before them the task of completing the military defeat of Fascist Germany.

In order to accomplish this, Poland and Czechoslovakia had to be completely liberated and the German Fascists had to be dealt the final blow on their own territory. This was an extraordinarily difficult task. Huge enemy fortifications, which had been built over a period of many years and even decades, would have to be stormed. The Fascists, sensing their approaching end, fought with the desperation of the doomed. And besides, the Hitler command still had at its disposition important forces, and as before they were maintaining the majority of these on the Soviet-German front.

Two hundred and four enemy divisions, 180 of them German, fought against the Red Army. On the Western Front fewer than seventy German divisions opposed the Anglo-American troops. However, even with these forces, the Hitler command was able to organize, at the end of December, 1944, a counter-attack on the Western Front in the Ardennes, which put the Anglo-American troops in a very difficult position.

On 6 January, 1945, the English Prime Minister, Winston Churchill, addressed to the Soviet Government a letter in which he sketched the situation in the West and the Allies' serious position, and asked for help.

The Red Army, faithful in its duty to its allies, launched a large-scale offensive on a broad front from the Baltic to the Carpathians, a distance of 1,200 kilometres. This offensive was launched on 12 January, 1945, whereas it had actually been planned to begin later, on 20 January. On that very day the German command cut short their attack on the Western Front and began to throw divisions from the West with all speed into the battle on the Eastern Front.

The troops of the 1st Ukrainian front, commanded by Marshal Konev, achieved in a brilliant manœuvre the liberation of the whole of Silesia, advanced as far as the River Oder, forced a swift crossing of the river and by the end of February had reached the River Neisse.

On 14 January the 1st Byelorussian front, commanded by Marshal Zhukov, passed to the attack. On 17 January the troops of this front, together with the 1st Polish Army, freed Warsaw, the capital of Poland. Developing this rapid offensive, they surrounded and, at the end of February, exterminated a large concentration of enemy troops in the area around the town of Poznan; they then reached the River Oder, forced a crossing near Kustrin and created a springboard on the west bank of the Oder, 60 kilometres from Berlin. Soviet troops were now in possession of all the territory from the Vistula to the Oder.

In January, 1945, the troops of the 2nd Byelorussian front, commanded by Marshal Rokossovsky, and the 3rd Byelorussian front, commanded by General Chernyakhovsky, passed to the offensive in East Prussia. They fought their way through to the Baltic coast and cut off the whole East Prussian concentration of enemy troops. As a result a new East Prussian pocket was formed, in which dozens of Fascist divisions continued to offer resistance, but with absolutely no hope. The enemy offered especially stubborn resistance in the Koenigsberg region. In the course of these battles the officer commanding the front was killed on 18 February. This was General Chernyakhovsky, who had twice been awarded the title of Hero of the Soviet Union. Marshal Vasilyevsky was appointed to the post of front commander. On 9 April the troops on this front stormed and captured the town and fortress of Koenigsberg.

In the forty days of the 1945 winter offensive, the Red Army drove out the German Fascist troops from three hundred towns, took more than 2,400 railway stations, seized about a hundred munitions factories and took prisoner more than 350,000 of the enemy officers and men. In the course of the offensive Soviet troops, together with the Polish army, freed Poland from the Fascist occupying forces, restored to the Polish people the lands in the west which had originally been theirs and which had been seized by Germany. The friendship between the Soviet and Polish peoples was strengthened by ties of blood in their combined struggle against the common enemy—Hitler's Germany. On 21 April, 1945, the Soviet-Polish Treaty of friendship, mutual aid and post-war co-operation was signed to last over a period of twenty years.

The Storming and Capture of Berlin

The Red Army now had the task of capturing Berlin and inflicting the final defeat on the Hitler forces. The German command gathered almost the whole of its forces for the defence of Berlin—about a million soldiers, 10,000 guns and mortars, 1,500 tanks and self-propelling weapons, and 3,300 aircraft. The area between the Oder and Berlin was completely blocked by three huge defensive fortifications. Deep anti-tank ditches, endless rows of granite blocks, hundreds of minefields barred the path to the Soviet troops. Berlin had been transformed into a tremendous fortress.

For the assault on the German capital the Soviet command had concentrated 41,600 guns and 'Katyushas', 8,000 aircraft and 6,300 tanks. The attack on Berlin was made by troops commanded by Marshal Zhukov and Marshal Konev.

At dawn on 16 April the Soviet artillery directed a hurricane of fire against the enemy fortifications. Following the barrage of fire, the tanks moved forward to the attack, supported from the air by thousands of aircraft. Behind the tanks the infantry joined the attack.

The Hitlerites offered desperate resistance. Particularly fierce fighting took place on the Zeelovsky heights, where the enemy tried to launch a counter-attack. But here too the enemy's resistance was smashed. The defence put up by the German Fascist bloc was broken all along the front. On 21 April fighting was already going on in the suburbs of Berlin, and in a few days' time the troops of the 1st Byelorussian and the 1st Ukrainian fronts, meeting in the region of Potsdam, surrounded all the enemy forces in Berlin. On the River Elbe units of the 1st Ukrainian front met up with units of the 1st American Army.

The surrounded German Fascist troops continued their resistance. For ten days, fierce fighting did not cease by day or night in the streets of Berlin. Every house was brought into the battle.

On 30 April the Soviet troops who had broken through into the centre of Berlin began to storm the Reichstag building. On the night preceding 1 May two regimental sergeants of the Intelligence Corps, M. Yegorov and M. Kantariya, hoisted the Victory Banner over the Reichstag. On 2 May the Berlin garrison surrendered. Hitler committed suicide. The Soviet troops took prisoner more than 300,000 German soldiers and officers in the Berlin region. In a few days Germany acknowledged defeat. On 8 May in Berlin representatives of the German High Command signed the act of unconditional surrender. The supreme power in Germany had passed to the governments of the Allied Powers.

The Potsdam Conference

The third conference of the governments of the USSR, the USA and England was held in Potsdam (near Berlin) from

17 July to 2 August. Participating in these deliberations were Stalin, Truman, who had stepped into the post of President of the USA after the death of Roosevelt in April, 1945, and Churchill, who was replaced during the workings of the conference by Attlee, who had become Prime Minister of Great Britain following the Labour victory in the Parliamentary elections.

The conference worked out the principles underlying the policy the allies were to adopt towards Germany. The agreement stipulated the necessity for the complete disarmament of Germany, the rooting out of Fascism and the reshaping of the political life of the country on a democratic pattern.

At the conference it was laid down that the Western frontier of Poland should follow the Oder-Neisse line. Thus Poland regained the lands that had been seized in the past by the Germans.

An International War Tribunal was created to sit in judgement on the chief Fascist war criminals. After the war grave crimes against humanity came to light and were laid bare. Once again the whole world could see how loathsome was the outlook of Fascism. The court severely punished the Fascist ringleaders.

CHAPTER XV

★

The Surrender of Japan and the Results of the Second World War

✳

Japanese Imperialism—the Enemy of the Soviet People

The Second World War had not ended with the defeat of Fascist Germany. Germany's ally in the Far East—imperialist Japan—continued to conduct military operations against China, the USA and England.

In spite of the Soviet-Japanese neutrality pact, Japan was in fact helping Germany in the war against the Soviet Union. In China, on the frontier with the USSR, Japan maintained the Kwantung army of crack troops, numbering more than a million. This forced the Soviet command, even in the most difficult days of the war, to maintain about forty divisions in the Far East. Japan tried to blockade from the sea the far-eastern frontiers of the USSR, and hampered by all possible means far-eastern shipping.

In the summer of 1942 Japanese ruling circles decided to enter upon a war against the Soviet Union. The Red Army's victory in the battle on the Volga foiled these treacherous plans. However, Japan continued to increase her forces in the Far East, while waiting for a convenient time to attack the USSR. Because of these hostile actions of the Japanese militarists, the Soviet Government abrogated the Soviet-Japanese neutrality agreement on 5 April, 1945.

In July, 1945, the USA, England and China demanded

Japan's unconditional surrender. When the Japanese Government answered this demand with a refusal, the Soviet Government, true to its obligation as an ally, associated itself with the declaration of the other three powers and announced that from 9 August the USSR would be in a state of war with Japan. By taking this decision the Soviet Government showed its resolve to bring the Second World War to an end, to put an end to the sufferings of the Chinese and of the other nations of the East, and to guarantee the security of the Soviet frontiers in the Far East.

The Defeat of the Kwantung Army and the Surrender of Japan

On 9 August, 1945, Soviet troops in the Far East with forces drawn from three fronts launched an offensive against the Kwantung Army. Along the coast of Korea, Sakhalin and the Kurile Islands, the ships of the Pacific Fleet joined the offensive. At the same time the troops of the People's Republic of Mongolia entered upon hostilities. On the first day of the offensive our troops broke through the enemy defences and advanced into the territory of Manchuria and Korea.

By dealing crushing blows from three directions at once the Soviet troops broke up the Kwantung Army and defeated its units separately. The defeated units of the Japanese army began to give themselves up.

By the end of August the Red Army had freed from Japanese imperialism the north-eastern province of China (Manchuria), Southern Sakhalin, the Kurile Islands and North Korea.

On the eve of the Soviet Union's entry into the war against Japan, American aircraft, at the command of President Truman of the USA, dropped two atomic bombs, on 6 and 9 August, on the Japanese cities of Hiroshima and Nagasaki, killing and maiming a quarter of a million of the inhabitants. This was a barbaric example of the use of an atomic weapon, not provoked by military necessity. By dropping the bombs on the Japanese cities, the US imperialists were trying to frighten the whole world, especially the Soviet Union. It marked the beginning of the aggressive course steered by the USA towards the establishment of world domination.

Japan had lost its crack Kwantung Army; it had suffered defeat at sea and had lost vast numbers of men in the struggle against the freedom-loving peoples of China, Korea, Indo-China, Indonesia and Burma. She had definitely lost the war and was forced to sign an act of unconditional surrender on 2 September, 1945. Thus was the breeding-ground of aggression in the Far East completely liquidated, and the Second World War came to an end.

The Main Results of the Second World War

The war, which had lasted six years, ended with the complete military defeat of the Fascist aggressors. The Soviet Union had been the main factor in the anti-Fascist coalition and had played a decisive role in achieving victory. Soviet armed forces, in the course of the war, had destroyed $506\frac{1}{2}$ German divisions and 100 divisions belonging to German satellites. The Allies, however, destroyed no more than 176 divisions. In the war against the USSR Germany had lost 10,000,000 men, which made up three-quarters of its overall losses in the Second World War.

The war had extremely important social and economic consequences. The Fascist defeat fundamentally changed the 'alignment of forces' in the international field. The whole world became convinced of the durability and great life force inherent in the socialist system. The authority of the USSR was immeasurably increased, and the role of the land of the Soviets was strengthened in deciding international questions.

The conditions had now been created for the transformation of socialism into a world-wide system. Socialism spread beyond the confines of one country and embraced a whole string of nations in Europe and Asia; this led to radical changes in the international situation.

By defeating Hitler's Germany, the Soviet Nation saved mankind from annihilation or enslavement by German Fascism, and preserved world civilization. This great exploit of Soviet citizens will never fade from the memory of a grateful mankind.

APPENDIX

★

Introduction

★

This section of the book deals with the three most controversial actions of the Soviet Union in the period 1939–45: the signing of the Stalin-Hitler Pact 1939, the Russo-Finnish War 1940–41 and the Russian refusal to help the insurgents in the Warsaw Uprising.

These three actions have often been presented in the West as convincing proof of Russia's villainy and so it is difficult for us to imagine how the Soviet Union could justify its behaviour in these cases—behaviour which appears to offend *any* code of moral conduct. To help the reader understand the extent of the gulf between the two viewpoints, I have summarized the Cold War or anti-Soviet positions on these events and placed them before the corresponding Russian versions. These summaries are not comments on the Soviet text nor are they necessarily my personal view. In effect they are the 'Western version'—the background against which the Russian version should be read.

The function of this section is to deal with the issues raised by the above events in much greater detail than in the main section of the book. To do this, I have drawn from sources other than Russian schoolbooks. To describe the Finnish campaign and the situation around Warsaw at the time of the Uprising, extracts have been taken from the memoirs of the Front commanders of those areas. For the Soviet view of the Stalin-Hitler pact and the political background of the war with Finland, I have used three books written for the Russian general public but which give quite lengthy assessments of Western policies and actions.

The selection and arrangement of the material from these sources follow the principles set out in the introduction. I have not included exact source references for each passage, but these are readily available through the publishers to any reader who needs them.

A

Negotiations between Britain, France and
the Soviet Union.
The Stalin-Hitler Pact

SUMMARY OF THE WESTERN POSITION

When Russia and Germany signed a 10-year Non-Aggression Pact on 23 August, 1939, the whole world was stunned. Ever since it came to power the Nazi Party had waged an uninterrupted anti-Soviet campaign, unequalled in virulence. The Nazis put themselves up as the sworn enemies of Bolshevism, dedicated to the destruction of the Soviet system.

Hitler and Stalin, who, for the previous decade, had been calling each other the most vile names, now completely disregarded the public opinion they had so carefully moulded and embraced one another. Their more sensitive followers received a profound shock.

For months before the signing of the pact Britain and France had been engaged with Russia in trying to draw up some sort of alliance that would effectively stop Hitler's war madness by surrounding him with overwhelming military power. Such a treaty might have been one way to prevent a European war. And yet while the British and French military missions were negotiating in Moscow, Russia was holding secret talks with Germany. Western countries regarded the signing of this amazing pact as an underhand betrayal of world peace. Sure enough, war followed one week later.

THE SOVIET VIEW

By the spring of 1939 a tense military and political situation had developed in Europe. Nazi Germany had gained key economic and military positions in the centre of the continent. Controversy raged among the ruling circles in Germany over where to strike next in the struggle for world power. Monopoly capital and the militarists were of like mind that the Soviet Union was the main obstacle to Germany's ambitious plans of conquest. It was only natural that the German Nazis made the Soviet Union, the world's first socialist country, an object of savage hatred. But they knew that a war against the Soviet Union would tax the strength of their armed forces and leave the German rear unprotected. Most of the Nazi policymakers believed, therefore, that it was advisable first to crush the weaker opponents of the bourgeois camp and then, having added to their strength through conquests in the West, to fall on their main adversary, the Soviet Union.

The Germans renounced the Anglo-German Naval Agreement of 1935 and the 1934 non-aggression pact with Poland. Hitler demanded the incorporation of Danzig into Germany.

Nazi Germany's plans to attack Poland were now clear. Fearing that this might be a prelude to German aggression westward, the British and French Governments undertook urgent measures to safeguard themselves and to exert pressure on Germany. They guaranteed assistance to Poland in case of attack, but this had no significant effect in lessening Germany's aggressive posture. In a further attempt to bring pressure to bear on Germany, Britain and France started negotiations with the USSR in March, 1939, on joint measures against Germany.

The Soviet Union was sincerely eager to establish a united front of Governments and peoples against German aggression. It wished to conclude an effective agreement with Britain and France, guaranteeing the security of Central and Eastern Europe and stipulating the form and extent of mutual and immediate assistance in the event of aggression. The USSR therefore agreed to negotiate with Britain and France.

With peace vital to the fulfilment of its great construction plans, the Soviet Union tried sincerely to reach agreement. The British and French Governments, however, hoped to saddle the Soviet Union with commitments which would inexorably draw the USSR into a war with Germany. In the event of Germany's turning westward the British and French hoped to secure Soviet aid, while avoiding any commitment themselves, should the Soviet Union be attacked. These proposals naturally were rejected by the Soviet Union, first because they contained no principle of reciprocity with regard to the Soviet Union and, second, because they contained guarantees limited only to Poland and Rumania while the Soviet Union's north-western frontiers with Finland, Estonia and Latvia were left unprotected.

The British and French proposals could not serve as a basis for organizing collective resistance against the further spread of aggression in Europe. The Anglo-French consent to negotiate with the Soviet Union was thus no more than a move in a dual game, a projection, in a new guise, of the Munich policy.

By dangling the prospect of an agreement with the Soviet Government before the Germans, the British and French hoped to induce them to sign a far-reaching agreement, one that would not tread on the toes of the British and French monopolies in world markets but would ensure a German assault on the Soviet Union.

The British and French Governments were insincere in the extreme and doubly so because Anglo-French attempts were simultaneously made to obtain closer contacts with Germany. Secret Anglo-German talks took place in London in June–August, 1939, concerning agreements formalizing an alliance against the Soviet Union. During these talks, the British spokesman, Minister Robert Hudson, told his German opposite number, Helmuth Wolthat, that if Britain and Germany were to come to terms, broad opportunities would arise for their two countries in the British Empire and in China and Russia. Hudson stressed specially that in Russia 'there was a possibility for Germany to take part in vast activities'. This was as much as saying that Britain was eager to slice up the world between herself and Germany, prodding Germany to engage in economic expansion and also attack the USSR.

Right-wing Labour leaders backed the policy of connivance with the Nazis. Late in July, 1939, secret conversations took place between Theodor Kordt, Councellor of the German Embassy in London, and Labour leader Charles Buxton, who approved the scheme to demarcate spheres of influence. He told Kordt that if Germany promised to stay out of Empire affairs, Britain would be willing to respect German interests in East and South-East Europe, to abandon the guarantees it had given certain countries, to induce France to break its mutual assistance treaty with the USSR, and to break off negotiations with the Soviet Union. Some other Labour leaders were solidly behind Buxton. Bevin made the proposal at a Labour Party conference to 'pool the great resources of the world' and offer Germany, Italy and Japan 'a place in the sun'.

Though every minute counted, Britain and France employed dilatory tactics in the talks with the USSR, and to speed them up the Soviet Government suggested parleys by military missions of the three countries in Moscow. The suggestion was accepted, and a French delegation came to London in order to depart for Moscow jointly with the British. This was when Ivan Maisky, Soviet Ambassador to Britain, had a very revealing talk with the head of the British delegation to Moscow. Here is Maisky's record of it:

'I: "Tell me, Admiral, when are you leaving for Moscow?"

Reginald E. Drax: "That hasn't been settled, but in the next few days."

I: "You are flying, of course? Time is precious: the atmosphere in Europe is extremely tense."

Drax: "Oh no! We of the two delegations, including the technical personnel, are about 40, and there is the luggage . . . It would be inconvenient to fly."

I: "If flying is unsuitable, perhaps you will go to the Soviet Union in one of your fast cruisers? . . . That would be forceful and impressive—military delegations aboard a warship . . . Besides, it would not take too long from London to Leningrad."

Drax (with a sour expression): "No, a cruiser won't do either. If all of us were to go aboard a cruiser, we should have to evict several dozen of its officers and take their place in their cabins . . . Why cause any inconvenience? No, no, we shan't go by cruiser." '

What happened, however, was that the delegations left London as late as 5 August, 1939, aboard a combined freighter-passenger ship doing 13 knots and arriving in Leningrad on 10 August.

The talks lasted from 12 to 21 August. There were nine meetings in all. At the very first meeting it became obvious that the British and French missions were not empowered to sign any military agreement. Moreover, while the Soviet delegation was headed by the People's Commissar of Defence and included top-ranking representatives of the Soviet Armed Forces, the British and French delegations were made up of second-level officials who lacked the authority to decide vital military issues.

One of the central issues discussed during the negotiations was that of military plans. At the first meeting K. Y. Voroshilov bluntly asked whether the British and French missions had such plans. The Anglo-French side tried to evade the issue and sought to limit themselves to outlining three general principles which the French General Doumenc formulated as follows: 1) creation of two stable fronts in the west and east against the enemy, 2) continuity of the front, 3) employment of all forces against the enemy. But these principles were too abstract and did not commit anyone to anything. 'We have gathered here,' declared the head of the Soviet military mission, 'not to adopt a general declaration but to work out a concrete military convention which should stipulate the number of divisions, artillery pieces, tanks, aircraft, naval squadrons, and so forth for joint participation in the defence of the contracting powers.'

While the head of the French mission presented, if only in general outline, his General Staff's plan of military operations, the British side said nothing definite and did not report on any operational plan for the British Army. Neither was anything said about the operational plan of the joint Anglo-French Navy.

In contrast to the British and French delegations, the Soviet side pursued the definite goal of uniting the efforts of the USSR, Britain and France in the struggle against Nazi Germany's aggression. The Soviet delegation set out a plan of military operations envisaging the participation of the armed forces of the contracting states. Chief of the General Staff B. M. Shaposhnikov outlined a plan for the deployment of the Soviet Armed Forces on the western frontiers of the USSR, and three versions of a plan of military operations.

The first version detailed measures to be taken in the event of Nazi Germany attacking Britain and France, the second dealt with a German attack on Poland and Rumania and the third with a German attack on the USSR using the territories of Finland, Estonia and Latvia. These plans specified the exact number of Red Army infantry and cavalry divisions that would be used, the number of heavy guns, tanks and war planes, and the projected areas for the movement of troops. These concrete plans showed the Soviet Government's resolute desire to eliminate the threat of Nazi aggression, avert war and thus save millions of human lives as well as prevent the destruction of enormous material values.

The Soviet delegation made it perfectly clear that the USSR would take part in hostilities only on condition that its Armed Forces would be allowed to pass through Poland and Rumania. This demand was fully justified. In the absence of a common frontier with Germany, the USSR could fulfil its commitments to the Allies only if its troops would be permitted to pass through the territory of states requiring protection from Nazi aggression. The head of the Soviet delegation, K. Y. Voroshilov, declared that unless there would be a positive reply to this cardinal question of the transit of Soviet troops through the territory of Poland in the areas of Wilno and Galicia and across the territory of Rumania, further negotiations would be futile and would have no real significance.

The Anglo-French mission found itself in a difficult position on the issue of the passage of Soviet troops through Poland and Rumania. This problem became the stumbling block on the road to further negotiations. The British and French delegations knew that the transit of Soviet troops did not fit into their Governments' plans. Poland, which still nourished hopes of evading attack from Germany, was also against allowing Soviet troops to cross her territory. Obviously it was useless to continue talks unless a reply would be forthcoming to the proposals advanced by the Soviet delegation. Accordingly they were suspended for three days, beginning 18 August. They were resumed on the 21st only to be broken off completely after it was learned that the British and French Governments had sent no reply and their missions had requested a postponement of another three or four days.

In this connection the Soviet military mission issued an official written statement which said: 'The Soviet military mission cannot imagine how the Governments and General Staffs of Britain and France could have sent their missions to the USSR to negotiate a military convention without giving them precise and positive instructions on such an elementary issue as the transit and actions of Soviet Armed Forces against the troops of the aggressor on the territories of Poland and Rumania with whom Britain and France have corresponding political and military agreements. Considering, however, that the French and the British are turning this axiomatic issue into a great problem requiring lengthy study, it stands to reason that there are many grounds for doubting their desire for active and serious military co-operation with the USSR. In view of the above, responsibility for the procrastination of the military talks as well as for their interruption naturally lies with the French and British sides.'

The Soviet Government had worked resolutely to establish a powerful coalition against the aggressor. There was every possibility to curb the Nazi aggression for in the summer of 1939 the armed forces of the three contracting powers and Poland were considerably superior to the armed forces of Germany and Italy.

Referring to developments on the eve of the Second World War, Western reactionary writers rehash the lie that the USSR had betrayed the cause of collective resistance against the aggressor, that Russia had betrayed her allies (Britain and France) by concluding an agreement with Hitler. They spread the version that the causes of the Second World War should be sought not in the policies of the Fascist states and the imperialist powers, but in the policy of the Soviet Government which, they allege, had refused to meet the Western Governments half-way.

Professor Beloff of Oxford University claims that the Soviet-German rapprochement was the result of a prolonged and consistent foreign policy of the USSR. US historian Watson writes that in 1939 the Soviet Union sought to set Germany and the Western Powers at loggerheads and for this reason concluded an 'aggressive' non-aggression pact with her.

Winston Churchill bluntly stated that Russia 'pursued the policy of an arrangement with Germany at the expense of Poland' and that 'a "Fourth Partition of Poland" was to be the basis of the German-Russian rapprochement'. He quoted M. Daladier as writing that 'the USSR had conducted two negotiations, one with France, the other with Germany. She appeared to prefer to partition rather than to defend Poland. Such was the immediate cause of the Second World War.'

Slanderous fabrications of this sort are widely disseminated by the bourgeois press.

In spite of the peaceful character of the Soviet Union's pre-war foreign policy and the fact that it was permeated with the desire to avert war, bourgeois reactionary literature gives it an utterly false colouring.

What was the actual state of Soviet-German relations at that tense period?

In May, 1939, Hitler's diplomats in Moscow and Berlin began to explore possibilities for improving relations between Germany and the USSR. In that month two important officials of the German Foreign Ministry approached G. A. Astakhov, Soviet Chargé d'Affaires in Berlin, on two separate occasions and pointed out that the German press had altered its tenor and ceased hostile attacks against the Soviet Union. It also assured him that Germany harboured no aggressive designs against the USSR. Both in Berlin and in Moscow Germany intensified its efforts to achieve a rapprochement with the USSR. In Moscow Count von der Schulenburg, the German Ambassador, spoke with Deputy Commissar for Foreign Affairs V. P. Potyomkin and outlined a concrete plan for improving German-Soviet relations. He believed that this could be achieved in three stages: namely, by concluding a trade and credit agreement, normalizing press and cultural relations and, finally, by improving political relations.

In Berlin on 3 August Germany's Foreign Minister Ribbentrop invited G. A. Astakhov to visit him and informed him of the German Government's decision to radically alter German-Soviet relations. At that time the Soviet Government still believed in the success of Anglo-French-Soviet talks and on 7 August informed Berlin that it could not accept the German proposals.

On 15 August Schulenburg urgently sought the consent of the Commissariat for Foreign Affairs for Ribbentrop to visit Moscow and have talks with Soviet Government leaders. Foreign Commissar Molotov in reply expressed the wish to improve relations with Germany but said that it was up to Germany to take serious practical steps in this direction. This message was immediately forwarded to Hitler who read it with irritation and sent a cable to Schulenburg demanding that he should 'arrange immediately another conversation with Molotov and do everything possible to see that this conversation takes place without any delay'.

On 20 August Hitler sent a cable to Stalin offering a non-aggression pact with the Soviet Union. At this critical time the Anglo-French refusal to conclude an agreement with the Soviet Union added to the tension in Europe. The world moved to the brink of a major military disaster. The only question still unanswered was where Germany would strike next. Much depended on the further alignment of forces in the world arena. The Soviet Union had to make a difficult choice. It could either attempt to reach a fresh agreement with Britain and France which it knew would fail, or accept Germany's offer of a non-aggression treaty. If the Soviet Union rejected the German proposal or dallied with the reply the balance could tilt against it, and this at a time when German aggression against the USSR had to be averted in order to frustrate the plans of a world 'crusade' against the socialist country, to eliminate the threat of the bloc whose creation had been discussed in Munich and to win time and build up defences. The Soviet Union therefore consented to the German proposals and on 23 August Ribbentrop arrived in Moscow by plane. Negotiations were opened immediately and the Soviet-German non-aggression pact for a ten-year period was signed in the evening of the same day. It was a non-aggression pact and not a 'friendship agreement' as it is sometimes portrayed in the West. Ribbentrop's suggestion to prefix the pact with a preamble about the friendly nature of Soviet-German relations was categorically rejected by Stalin who said in no uncertain terms that 'the Soviet Government could not honestly assure the public of the existence of friendly relations with Germany after they had been covered with pails of mud the past six years by the Nazi Government.'

The anti-Soviet slander later heaped upon the Soviet-German Treaty was based on the contention that after signing the Treaty the Soviet Union had allegedly altered its foreign policy and rejected collective security measures to combat Fascist aggression. This was untrue. Soviet foreign policy had for a long time been aimed at splitting the anti-Soviet front built in Munich. The Soviet Government had tried to do so by concluding an appropriate agreement with Britain and France and it was only after the Governments of these two countries sabotaged a favourable outcome that the Soviet Government tackled the task from the other end—through an agreement with Germany.

In the past there were complaints that the Soviet Union did not publish documents. Now they have been published, including the minutes of the Anglo-French-Soviet military talks. It seems that an unbiased person should now clearly see who sincerely worked to preserve peace and who played hide and seek. Nevertheless, Western writers continue to slander the Soviet Union.

In 1963 a book by Matthew P. Gallagher was published in the USA, claiming that the USSR precipitated the Second World War. Describing the stand of the USSR at the Anglo-French-Soviet talks in Moscow he says, 'If the Soviet leaders ever put stock in the feasibility and desirability of joint action with the West at this juncture, their expectations in this direction were short-lived, and from very early in the negotiations they took care to prepare an alternative line. In April, the Soviet Union began to take soundings in Berlin as to the possibility of achieving a *modus vivendi* with Germany. From that time on, Soviet policy began to probe for a German understanding, and while the British and French pressed more anxiously for some arrangement in the East, the Russians placed increasingly unacceptable conditions in the way of agreement. Finally, in the summer of 1939, while an Anglo-French military mission was actually in Moscow working for an understanding with the Soviet Union, the Soviet-German non-aggression pact was concluded. The non-aggression pact with Germany was negotiated behind the backs of the English and French—and at their expense.'

Published documents conclusively show that in the entire course of negotiations between the military delegations of the three states in Moscow the Soviet Government worked resolutely and consistently for an agreement with Britain and France and made no promises to Germany, nor conducted secret negotiations with her representatives. It patiently awaited a positive reply from the British and French Governments concerning the transit of Soviet troops across Polish and Rumanian territory. In the absence of such a stipulation no agreement would have been effective. The British and French Governments apparently expected the Soviet Union to wage war with Germany from the stratosphere but on no account to move its troops through Polish territory! Only when the talks had reached a stalemate did the Soviet Government consent to negotiate with Germany. It had no other alternative in this critical situation.

The conclusion of the Soviet-German non-aggression pact sharply changed the balance of forces in Europe and foiled the plans to involve the Soviet Union in a war in 1939. Amid an acute crisis in the relations between European states, when all efforts of the Soviet Union to organize collective resistance to Nazi expansion were blocked by Britain and France, it was necessary to avert the threat of war and to drive a wedge into the anti-Soviet bloc which the imperialist powers were secretly knocking together.

The British and French Governments, and with them the landowner-bourgeois Government of Poland, refused to conclude a defensive agreement with the USSR. Blind hatred for the world's first socialist state prevailed over common sense. They preferred another road, one which led them to war.

SOURCES:

The Secrets of the Second World War by G. Deborin. Translated by Y. Markov.

The Second World War by G. Deborin. Translated by V. Schneiersohn.

They Sealed Their Own Doom by P. Zhilin. Translated by D. Fidlon.

The above three titles were published by Progress Publishers, Moscow.

B

The Soviet-Finnish War
1940-41

SUMMARY OF THE WESTERN POSITION

Soon after Russia had annexed Eastern Poland, Estonia, Latvia and Lithuania were persuaded to sign a treaty which gave the Soviet Union the right to garrison troops in these states. As a result Russia gained military control of the whole area east of the Nazi-Soviet partition line.

The most vulnerable part of the Russian frontier was now in the region of Leningrad, on the border with Finland. The Russians tried to make Finland agree to territorial alterations which would push the Finnish border further away from Leningrad. This would increase Russia's security, should she be attacked through Finland, but would of course equally decrease Finland's security. In this area Finland had built strong defensive fortificaⁱions known as the 'Mannerheim Line'. This barrier would have to be surrendered in the proposed adjustments of territory. Russia also required Finland to lease Petsamo, her only northern port, and the port of Hangö on the edge of the Gulf of Finland for use as a Russian naval and air base. This port together with the Estonian port of Paldiski (now in Soviet hands) would dominate the Gulf of Finland. Coastal batteries built at these two ports would ensure complete Russian control of sea traffic over a long stretch of Finnish coastline—and one which included Helsinki and Viborg, the two largest Finnish cities.

The negotiations concerning these matters had started on 12 October, 1939, but became deadlocked on 13 November when the Finnish delegation gave way on all Russian demands but one: they would not lease Hangö.

Thereafter an anti-Finnish campaign was started in the Russian press. On 28 November the Soviet Government officially denounced the 1932 Soviet-Finnish non-aggression pact (which provided for six months' notice of denunciation). On 29 November Molotov announced the breaking off of diplomatic relations between the two countries. He described as a 'perfidious calumny' Western news reports that Russia intended to violate Finnish independence or annex territory. On 30 November Russian bombers raided Helsinki and a number of other towns.

Russian armour and troops crossed the Finnish border *en masse* at points along its entire length.

Western countries reacted with shock and disgust to this brutal and bullying attack. The British National Council of Labour, a body hardly likely to react with stereotyped anti-Soviet utterances, had this to say: 'The British trade union and Labour movement views with profound horror and indignation the Soviet Government's unprovoked attack upon a small state with whom it had made a pact of non-aggression . . . Soviet imperialism has revealed itself as using the same methods as the Nazi power . . . We regard with deep detestation the action of the Soviet Government, because it has in the past professed to be the leader of the world's working class movement, guardian of the rights of peoples against their oppressors, interpreter of socialist principles, and the custodian of international peace. British Labour, in the light of recent events, repudiates utterly these claims.'

Quite unexpectedly the small but well trained Finnish Army carried out a highly skilled and effective defence. The Russian Bear received a bloody nose.

The reality behind this journalist's phrase meant that tens of thousands of bewildered peasants in Red Army uniform were left to freeze, bleed or starve to death in Finnish forests. The blundering ineptitude of the initial attacks had left the Russian infantry without protection from their tanks or artillery. These had been immobilized by a combination of deep snow, difficult terrain and well-laid ambushes by Finnish ski-troops. These troops would disappear into the trees before the Russians could bring up reinforcements. The Finns would then move to the rear of the Red Army divisions and cut off their supply routes.

Soviet political and military prestige sank to its lowest point. On 14 December Russia was formally expelled from the League of Nations.

THE SOVIET VIEW

I

The Political Background

The German invasion of Poland and the rapid eastward drive of the Nazi troops indicated that the Hitler Government was out to occupy suitable positions on the Soviet border for a subsequent attack. There was no guaranteeing that Hitler, intoxicated by his successes in Poland and prodded on by the Western Powers, would postpone the assault on the Soviet Union. The Polish developments constituted an extreme danger for the USSR. The situation called for rapid and vigorous action.

In September, 1939, the Soviet Union took the due preventive measures—reservists in some military areas were called to arms, troops were relocated, etc. But this was obviously insufficient. The German drive eastward had to be blocked. The Nazis could not be allowed to reach the Soviet border. Nor could the Soviet people be indifferent to the lot of their brothers—the oppressed West Ukrainian and Byelorussian minorities in Poland, who were abandoned to their fate by the Polish rulers.

This was why, in pursuance of its liberation mission, the Soviet Army marched into the Western Ukraine and Western Byelorussia, where it was enthusiastically welcomed by the population.

Hitler's road eastward was blocked. He had to call a halt.

Throughout October, 1939, democratic elections were held in the newly-liberated areas to people's assemblies. Acting on the will of the people, these assemblies proclaimed Soviet power in the territories under their jurisdiction and requested the Supreme Soviet of the USSR to admit Western Ukraine and Western Byelorussia into the fraternal family of Soviet nations. The Supreme Soviet complied. Western Ukraine and Western Byelorussia were reunified with the Ukrainian and Byelorussian Soviet Socialist Republics respectively.

The German invasion of Poland also added to the danger of a Nazi attack on the Soviet Union from the Baltic shore. The bourgeois Baltic republics did not have the resources to offer Hitler any resistance. What was more, the success of German arms in Poland had stimulated pro-Hitler elements in those republics. There was the danger that they would become German vassal states and bridgeheads for an attack on the Soviet Union. In view of this, the Soviet Government approached the Baltic Governments with the offer of mutual assistance treaties.

The Soviet proposals were met favourably by the peoples of those countries, and their Governments gave their consent. Estonia was the first to sign, on 28 September, 1939, followed by Latvia on 5 October and Lithuania on 10 October. Under the terms of these treaties the Soviet Union and the Baltic republics undertook to render each other aid, military aid included, in the event of an attack or threat of attack by any great European power. Estonia and Latvia leased bases to the Soviet navy, air force and artillery, and Lithuania assigned areas where a stipulated strength of Soviet ground troops and air units could be stationed.

The treaties fortified the defences of the Soviet Union and the Baltic republics. The danger of the latter's conversion into imperialist anti-Soviet bridgeheads was averted. The Soviet defences were moved far to the west, and the Soviet navy acquired a number of important bases in the ice-free part of the Baltic Sea.

Now the Soviet Union had to consider the safety of its border with Finland, where the German Fascists and Anglo-French imperialists were assiduously making war preparations against the Soviet Union. Finland was being built up as a staging area for an attack on Leningrad and the Murmansk railway. The Finns had erected a powerful and deep system of long-term fortifications known as the Mannerheim Line. At many points in South and East Finland strategic railways and motor roads had been built to the Soviet border. The security of Leningrad, just 32 kilometres from the Finnish border, was in jeopardy.

The Soviet Government initiated negotiations with the Finns on 12 October, 1939. The talks proceeded with direct and unprecedented US interference.

On the day the talks began, the US President sent the Soviet Union and Finland a telegram in which he voiced the 'hope' that the negotiations would not culminate in an agreement curtailing the independence and sovereignty of Finland. In reply

110

M. I. Kalinin stated that the Soviet Government, which had declared Finnish independence in 1917, had no other aim but to consolidate Soviet-Finnish co-operation in matters of security. Hitler's Germany acted much like the US, British and French Governments. Its Minister to Helsinki insisted that the Finnish Government reject agreement with the USSR.

The Soviet Government repeatedly proposed to the Finnish Government that the issue be resolved in a mutually advantageous way: to move the frontier a few tens of kilometres further west of Leningrad in exchange for a much larger territory northwest of Lake Onega. But all to no avail. The Moscow proposal was rejected and our frontier guards received replies in the form of shots. What were the Finnish leaders banking on? Obviously, not on their own relatively small forces. They were encouraged by the promises of the imperialist powers to assist them with troops and equipment; they expected that an anti-Soviet bloc would be established; they were blinded by the nationalistic dream of a 'great Finland' extending from the Gulf of Bothnia to the White Sea and Lake Ilmen, and finally, they relied on the Mannerheim Line in the event of an unsuccessful offensive against Leningrad and the need to turn to the defensive.

The Finnish reactionaries, headed by Mannerheim, chose a policy of anti-Soviet provocations. Large Finnish forces were deployed on the Soviet border and bombarded Soviet units near Leningrad. Mannerheim wrote in his memoirs that he was sure the United States and Britain would intervene on his behalf.

Having provoked the Soviet-Finnish war, the imperialists of the United States, Britain and France sought to fan it into a general anti-Soviet crusade. American historians write that the prospect of such a crusade 'loomed as a god-given opportunity'. The imperialists decided to make use of the League of Nations.

On 14 December the Council declared the Soviet Union an 'aggressor' and 'expelled' it from the League of Nations. Only seven of the fifteen Council members, including the three deliberately elected for the purpose, voted for the 'expulsion'.

'Britain and France,' Tass news agency commented, 'with a population of 89 million, backed by Belgium, Bolivia, Egypt, the Union of South Africa and the Dominican Republic, with a total population of just 38 million, "expelled" the Soviet Union, which has a population of 183 million.'

The League of Nations, tainted by connivance with, and

abettment of, the Japanese, Italian and German aggressors, completed its own destruction by publicly approving and supporting the war provoked by the Finnish ruling class against the Soviet Union. It thereby signed its own death warrant.

The Soviet expulsion from the League of Nations was a manœuvre that helped the reactionaries, under cover of the League resolution, to multiply their assistance to the Finns and redouble their effort to turn the Second World War into an anti-Soviet crusade. The reactionary press hoped that Hitler's Germany would now turn its arms against the USSR and that events would lead up to a united front against the Soviet Union.

The Soviet–Finnish war was a hard war for the Soviet Union. The theatre of operations ruled out massive manœuvres and flanking movements, owing to the large number of lakes and the dense forests.

The situation was made more complicated still by the assistance lavished on Finland from abroad. It was not confined to arms and war material.

The flow of US, British and French arms to Finland increased. A Finland committee, headed by Herbert Hoover, was organized. The US Government granted a $10,000,000 loan to Finland, against which that country was supplied arms at give-away prices. The American banks also gave Finland a few loans. Volunteers flocked to enrolment centres in the USA and other capitalist countries for shipment to Finland.

A group of British Labour leaders toured Finland with Chamberlain's blessing, promising the Finns more aid and calling on them to fight the Soviet Union 'until victory is won'.

Britain and France hastened to use the League of Nations resolution to prepare a direct aggression against the Soviet Union. An attack was planned for 15 March, 1940, simultaneously in the Middle East against Baku, and in Finland. British and French troops were being massed for the assault in Syria and Iraq. On instructions of the French Government, General Gamelin worked out a detailed plan of operations, involving Turkey, Iraq, Rumania, Greece and Yugoslavia. General Weygand, who was in command of preparations on the spot, wrote:

'For my part, I consider it cardinal to twist the Soviet Union's neck in Finland . . . or elsewhere.'

Preparations for an attack on the Soviet Union from the Middle East began in the summer of 1939, that is, at the time when

Britain and France were still negotiating with the Soviet Union. Weygand arrived at his headquarters in Beirut on 31 August, 1939.

The British and French Governments also formed a special Expeditionary Corps for the northern attack against the USSR. The Corps was to be brought up via Sweden and Norway. The British Government requested Sweden and Norway to let the Anglo-French force cross their territory.

Early in January, the Soviet Government pointed out to the Swedish and Norwegian Governments that their conduct was in gross violation of their declared neutrality and stressed that 'the Swedish and Norwegian Governments are not putting up due resistance to the pressure of powers that seek to draw Sweden and Norway into a war with the USSR'. These warnings induced the Swedes and Norwegians to hold up their reply to the British and French demands for right of passage.

The US, British and French Governments opposed the conclusion of peace between Finland and the Soviet Union. On 28 December, the Finnish Government requested the United States to mediate an armistice. The American reply denounced the Finnish *démarche* and the very idea of a negotiated settlement.

In February, 1940, the Soviet Army breached the Mannerheim Line. In early March the Soviet troops swung round Viborg across the ice-locked Gulf of Finland, enveloped the city, emerged on the coast between Viborg and Helsinki, and marched on the Finnish capital. The Finnish Government was compelled to plead for an armistice, which it did through Sweden. The US, British and French Governments demanded that Finland fight on. Churchill, who came to Paris as First Lord of the Admiralty on instructions of the British Government, joined Daladier in telling a representative of the Finnish Government that there was no point in an armistice because Western action was about to begin. Norway and Sweden, he said, would not be requested this time, but ordered. Daladier informed Helsinki that Britain and France insisted on Finland's declining the Soviet peace proposals. 'I assure you once more,' he wrote, 'we are ready to give our help immediately. The airplanes are ready to take off. The operational force is ready.' The US Government declared that it would be glad 'to do what it could, short of mediation or actual involvement in the dispute'.

The Finnish War Council studied the statements on 7 March

and decided to accept the Soviet peace terms. The Soviet-Finnish Peace Treaty was signed on 12 March, 1940. The policymakers of the United States, Britain and France received word of it with obvious displeasure.

Military operations ceased. The signatories undertook to refrain from the use of arms against each other and from entering into any alliances and coalitions aimed against the other party. Finland pledged, as provided for in the 1920 Peace Treaty, to keep no submarines and no air forces in its waters along the Arctic coast, and to maintain only surface warships of limited tonnage. The Soviet-Finnish border was moved 150 kilometres away from Leningrad, and the Karelian Isthmus with Viborg, the Bay of Viborg and the islands in that bay were ceded to the Soviet Union. The western and northern shore of Lake Ladoga also became part of the Soviet Union. The safety of Murmansk and the Murmansk railway was secured by the transfer to the USSR of an area east of Merkjärvi, the town of Kuolajärvi and the formerly Finnish parts of the Rybachy and Sredny peninsulas. Lastly, Finland granted a thirty-year lease of the Hangö Peninsula with the adjoining islands and waters at the entrance to the Gulf of Finland for a Soviet naval base. The Soviet-Finnish war was over.

II

The Campaign

On 26 November I received an urgent report that the Finns had opened artillery fire on Soviet frontier guards near the village of Mainila killing four and wounding nine men. Ordering the troops of the Leningrad Military District to assume control over the Soviet-Finnish frontier along its entire length I immediately transmitted the message to Moscow. Instructions came to prepare a counter-attack. I was given a week to make ready but in effect the time was reduced to four days because Finnish detachments crossed the frontier at several points, and infiltrated groups of saboteurs behind our lines. The Soviet Government issued an official statement and at 0800 hours on 30 November, regular Red Army Forces launched operations to repel the anti-Soviet actions and the Soviet-Finnish war was on.

Orders were given to throw the enemy back from Leningrad, ensure the security of the frontier in Karelia and the Murmansk Region and force the puppet of the imperialist powers to refrain from any further provocations against the USSR. The main objective of the Soviet troops was the liquidation of the Finnish bridgehead on the Karelian Isthmus.

Finland's armed forces were commanded by Field-Marshal Baron von Mannerheim, former lieutenant-general of the Tsar's entourage, executioner of the Finnish Revolution of 1918 and sworn enemy of the Soviet Union since the October Revolution. With the help of foreign money, foreign equipment and local manpower, foreign engineers under his control built a heavily fortified permanent defence line in the Finnish part of the Karelian Isthmus. Judging from press reports, the Mannerheim Line was similar to the German Siegfried Line and the French Maginot Line.

The first fortifications were built between 1920 and 1929. Construction was resumed in 1938 and new fortifications were completed by the summer of the following year. Particular publicity was given to the so-called 'million' (in view of their cost) permanent gun emplacements and defence centres, but no details about the Mannerheim Line were published. Some of our reconnaissance officers, according to the documents that were sent to the Leningrad Military District, believed that even this line was nothing more than propaganda. But time showed how grossly they had erred.

Before the commencement of operations I once again asked Moscow for intelligence information and as before received reports which later proved to be incorrect because they under-estimated the actual strength of the Mannerheim Line. This, unfortunately, created many difficulties for us, and the Red Army learned the actual strength of the Mannerheim Line only when it was right up against it. At the time we were planning an army operation involving nine divisions and three tank brigades. Thus began the first stage of the campaign that lasted until 9 February and which in its turn was divided into several sub-stages. First we had to breach the security zone with its ramified system of multirow obstacles consisting of numerous barbed-wire entanglements, ditches and earthworks. Its approaches were covered by tank traps and defended by troops manning pillboxes and, more often, bunkers reinforced with logs and earth, and other defensive

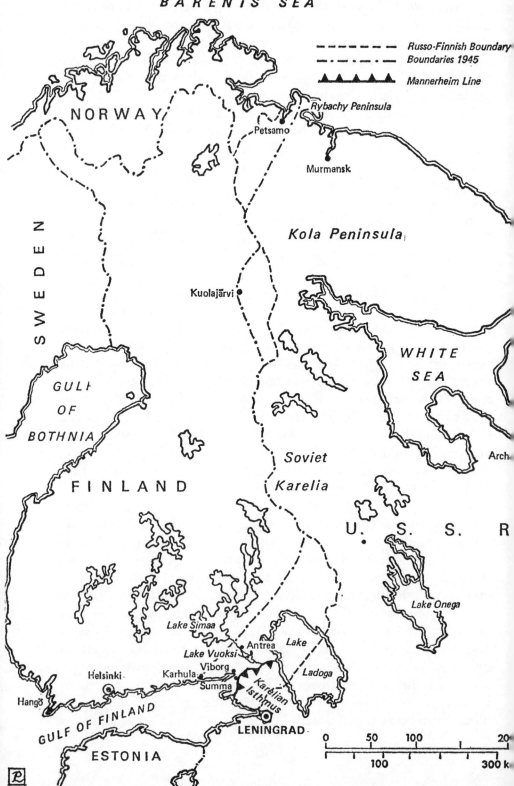

BARENTS SEA

	Russo-Finnish Boundary
	Boundaries 1945
▲▲▲▲	Mannerheim Line

NORWAY

Rybachy Peninsula

Petsamo

Murmansk

Kola Peninsula

SWEDEN

Kuolajärvi

WHITE

SEA

GULF

OF

BOTHNIA

Arch.

FINLAND

Soviet

Karelia

U. S. S. R

Lake Onega

Lake Simaa

Antrea   Lake

Lake Vuoksi

Helsinki   Viborg   Ladoga

Karhula

Hangö   Summa

Karelian Isthmus

GULF OF FINLAND

LENINGRAD

0   50   100   20

ESTONIA

100   300 k

℗

installations. But it was the minefields that gave us the greatest trouble in the beginning.

There were all sorts of mines: anti-personnel, anti-tank and high-explosive, as well as booby traps. The retreating Finns evacuated all civilians, slaughtered or drove away the domestic cattle and laid waste to the entire territory. Bicycles, suitcases, gramophones, watches, wallets, cigarette cases and radios were scattered on the ground in villages and on the roads. To all appearances they had been discarded in haste. But at the first touch they would explode. Danger lurked everywhere. Stairs, porches, wells, tree-stumps, forest paths, the edges of woods and roads were all mined. The army was sustaining losses and the men were afraid to advance. Something had to be done promptly or the entire operation would collapse. Yet we had no effective defence against mines and were absolutely unprepared for such a contingency.

Zhdanov and I consulted several Leningrad engineers, including a group of instructors headed by Professor N. M. Izyumov from the Military Academy of Communications. We described the situation and said that we needed mine detectors. Thinking it over they said that it could be done and asked how much time they had. Zhdanov replied: 'Twenty-four hours.'

'Twenty-four hours? But that's impossible.'

'Impossible, yet it has to be done. The troops are in great difficulty. The success of the war depends on your invention.'

The engineers and instructors left us excited and somewhat nonplussed. But on the following day the first model of the mine detector was ready. It was tested, approved and put into line production. The advancing troops were preceded by an unbroken chain of sappers with mine detectors who went over every square metre of territory. Hearing the signal in their earphones they would warn the troops and then set off the mine. This considerably slowed up our advance but it guaranteed the safety of the troops. No longer afraid of the mines they waded through the snowdrifts disregarding the cold ($-45°$ C) and the icy, biting wind, constantly on the alert for Finnish snipers nesting in the high trees behind our lines.

By 12 December, the security zone covering the main sector of the Mannerheim Line was breached. After a swift reconnaissance in force we made an attempt to break through on the march but failed. During our artillery bombardment the Finns quitted their trenches and moved closer to the wire entanglements. But when our artillery began shelling the wire entanglements to open way for the troops, the Finns returned to their trenches. Imagining that our forces had already broken into the enemy trenches and were being shelled by our artillery, D. G. Pavlov, commander of our tank force, telephoned Voroshilov who ordered to cease the artillery barrage. Valuable time was lost in clarifying the situation and we were unable to break through on the heels of the enemy. The moment was lost.

Incidentally, a subsequent thorough investigation revealed that the artillery fire was directed mainly at the field defences between the pillboxes to soften up the enemy. The pillboxes stood undamaged. They were not subjected to direct fire, the only way they could be destroyed. Consequently, not a single pillbox was smashed at the time. That meant that our troops would not have been able to advance without sustaining heavy casualties. Preparing for a new breakthrough we examined the recently negotiated security zone. At various sectors its depth ranged from 20 to 60 kilometres with field defences concentrated along the roads. There was only a small number of pillboxes but more than 800 bunkers. Military engineers estimated that it had tens of kilometres of anti-tank ditches, almost 100 kilometres of tank traps, more than 100 kilometres of obstructions, more than 200 kilometres of barbed-wire entanglements and almost 400 square kilometres of minefields. All this made us wonder what the main defensive zone would be like.

We made an unsuccessful assault on it after five days of preparations. We had neither the experience nor the means to surmount such defences, the likes of which we had never seen before. Enemy defences were not suppressed. His pillboxes were silent, but each time our tanks lunged forward the Finns opened up, scoring hits on their sides and rear, and cut off the infantry with machine-gun fire and the attack would peter out. In those days our tanks were not equipped with heavy guns and could not crush the enemy pillboxes. The best they could do was to block the embrasures with their hulls. We also learned that we should not launch an attack from a distance and, despite the deep snow, we had to bring the assault positions closer to the pillboxes. Too few breaches had been made in the engineering installations so the tanks had to crowd together and became an excellent target. There was a scarcity of field radios for the commanders to maintain operational control, and this led to unsatisfactory co-ordination of the various arms. Another drawback was the shortage of assault groups specially trained to smash pillboxes and bunkers. The air force, which bombed only the rear of the enemy defences, did little to help the land forces to surmount these obstacles.

Still our main difficulty was the pillboxes. Our shells just would not pierce them. Irritated by our failure to advance, Stalin pointed out that ineffective military actions could affect our policy. The whole world had its eyes on us and the prestige of the Red Army was the guarantee of the Soviet Union's security. If we should get stuck for long against such a weak adversary, we would be encouraging the imperialists to further their anti-Soviet efforts.

After reporting to Stalin in Moscow I was ordered to take direct charge of reconnaissance and discover the secret of the Finnish pillboxes. I sent reconnaissance parties in three directions. They established the location and the number of the pillboxes, but not how they were actually constructed. Summoning a military engineer with a group of sappers, I ordered him to penetrate behind the enemy lines, blow up a pillbox, examine its concrete cover and bring a piece of the concrete back. They fulfilled the assignment and we sent the sample to Moscow where a research institute established that Finnish pillboxes were made of cement-600.

That was why our light artillery could not smash them. Besides, we found out that the casemates of many pillboxes were reinforced with several layers of armour plate around the embrasures and that their concrete walls and protective covering were from one and a half to two metres thick. The whole structure, moreover, was covered with two or three metres of tightly packed earth.

Talking things over with Voronov we decided to destroy the pillboxes by direct fire from superheavy artillery. We moved several 203–280mm guns of the High Command's Reserve closer to the front line and opened up at point-blank range on the pillboxes and their embrasures. Things started to move at once, and I then took measures to improve the co-ordination between the different arms of the service.

It was in that period that I, as Army Commander, was first issued a personal radio station. We were the first to fix the composition of assault groups for capturing and blowing up pillboxes. This experience was subsequently widely applied in breaching fortified areas during the Great Patriotic War. We also sent aircraft on reconnaissance missions over the Mannerheim Line. This took up the whole of January. Finally, by the beginning of February, we had maps of the enemy's defences, and could draw up an effective plan of breaching them. Stalin summoned Zhdanov and me to Moscow. I reported the plan in the presence of Molotov, Voroshilov, Timoshenko, Voronov and Grendal. The plan was approved.

In the evening we had supper with Stalin. He and Molotov questioned us about the results of the reconnaissance and the details of the plan and outlined the political aspect of the operation. After supper Stalin said that there would be certain changes; all was not well in the far north and it was necessary to establish a centralized command directly in the zone of military operations, to bring in fresh units and determine the direction of the offensive. The 7th Army was to play the decisive role by carrying out the operational plan assigned to it. He said that it was essential at all costs to capture the Mannerheim Line before the spring floods. That was the basic objective.

The reorganization was effected at the close of the first phase of the war. The Leningrad Military District was transformed into the north-western front under Army Commander 1st Class S. K. Timoshenko with A. A. Zhdanov as member of the Military Council. Thus, instead of an army offensive operation, there was to be a front operation conducted primarily by the 7th and 13th Armies. Joining their flanks they were to deal the main blow in the direction of Summa and Viborg. The breakthrough frontage extended 40 kilometres from Lake Vuoksi to Karhula. The right flank of the 13th Army was to move to Kexholm and the left to push towards Antrea through Kiurjolja and Ristseppjalja. The 7th Army under my command was to advance with its right flank on Viborg (the most heavily defended direction in the enemy's defence system) through Kjamjarja and with its left on Maxlakhti. The 7th Army consisted of the 34th, 10th, 50th and 19th Infantry Corps each of three divisions. Moreover, it had an infantry machine-gun brigade, 11 artillery regiments, five tank brigades and two separate tank battalions. Nine divisions were to deal the main blow on the right flank west of Muolanjarvi and three were to strike an auxiliary blow on the left flank east of Karhula.

We had an average of 50 guns per kilometre of the Front.

Today mortars are taken into account when describing the fire density, but then mortars and submachine-guns were just coming into service, and not without first overcoming the apathy of some officials.

The air arm also received its assignment. By agreement with the Chief of the Front Air Force, Corps Commander Y. S. Ptukhin, a third of the Front's fighters, a quarter of the bombers and three-quarters of the night bombers were placed under the command of Corps Commander S. P. Denisov, Chief of the 7th Army's Air Force, for the purpose of softening up the enemy's main defences.

In breaching the fortified area at the approaches to Summa the experimental heavy KV tank equipped with a powerful gun showed up well. Designed and built at the Kirov Plant, it was tested in combat conditions by workers and engineers. They took it right through the fortified area, but the enemy artillery was unable to put it out of action although it was hit by several shells. In effect, it proved to be invulnerable at the time. The KV tank was a great achievement of our industry and greatly boosted the Red Army's fighting capacity. Since then I have held these combat vehicles in high regard and never lost the chance of having them at my disposal.

At about the same time we were reinforced by an infantry division, formerly a territorial unit, and a large cavalry unit. I shall return to the infantry division later. But as regards the cavalry it did not live up to expectations through the fault of its commander who had failed to lay in a supply of calked horseshoes and when the unit went into attack the horses slipped and fell on the ice. The attack broke down. But these were individual setbacks, for we had already advanced a long way in heavy battles.

The second stage of the campaign began with a powerful artillery preparation on 11 February, 1940. Six days later the main defence zone was breached despite the tenacious resistance of the Finns. In this operation particular credit should be given to the 123rd Infantry Division under Colonel F. F. Alyabushev. Eight kilometres in depth, this zone had more than twenty strongpoints, about 200 pillboxes and more than 1,000 bunkers. There was an average of two pillboxes and five bunkers interconnected by trenches and protected by various obstacles and a system of flank and oblique fire per kilometre of front and in the main directions in the defiles between lakes and swamps their density was several times greater.

Piercing the main zone, we fought our way through for several kilometres, overcame isolated positions and came up against a second defence line. Air reconnaissance reported that eight kilometres ahead there was still another defence line. It took us two weeks to break through them. But that was not all. At Viborg we encountered a fortified area consisting of two lines of perimeter defences. On top of that our reconnaissance reported that a canal linked the area with Lake Saimaa. It was already March and the slightest delay in our offensive would enable the Finns to flood the entire area.

T. F. Shtykov, member of the Army Military Council, and I went to the 70th Division. I ordered the Divisional Commander, M. P. Kirponos, to reconnoitre the Viborg Fortified Area during the night; in the meantime we would bring in an extra-heavy artillery regiment. Kirponos decided to bypass part of the fortifications from the north-west. Previously we had attempted this manœuvre by sending some troops across the ice, but their advance was blocked by ice breaks and several tanks sank. Kirponos on his own initiative tried this again. His men carried off all the enemy sentries without a sound. He then transferred his entire division to the western shore of the gulf. Returning the following morning I found the division gone. This happened on 4 March. Commending the 70th Division, I reinforced it and instructed Kirponos to advance on Viborg along the western shore and envelop the town from the rear. After that I reported the operation to Stalin.

The artillery opened point-blank fire. Virtually tearing through the enemy defences the 7th Army bore down on Viborg. Later Stalin phoned me and ordered the capture of the town within two or three days. The Mannerheim Line was left behind. Leningrad was far away and no longer threatened. We did not want much from the Finns, but to conclude peace it was necessary to show them that the road to Helsinki was open and that the fall of Viborg would be the last serious warning to them. On the other hand, any delay in bringing the war to a victorious conclusion would enable the French and the Swedes to send in reinforcements and instead of a war with one state we would have to fight against a coalition.

While I was talking to Stalin, our troops stormed Viborg. Now the way to Helsinki was open. Realizing that further resistance would be useless, the Finnish Government proposed negotiations. On 12 March, the terms of the peace treaty were approved and at 1200 hours on 13 March hostilities were terminated. The new frontier passed west of Viborg not far from where the Russian border had been in the middle of the 11th century during the reign of Prince Vladimir Yaroslavich.

The Party and the Government conferred deserved recognition on the men. Of the 9,000 officers and men who received military awards 405, including myself, were made Heroes of the Soviet Union. The awards were presented by Mikhail Kalinin, in May, 1940, in Viborg's Suvorov Square.

Before leaving for Moscow I spent a week examining the Mannerheim Line, although I had already looked it over before, while the officers of the Leningrad Military District made the required estimates. The total depth of the territory covered with defensive installations ranged from eighty to a hundred kilometres. Of these installations 350 were of reinforced concrete and 2,400 of logs and earth and excellently camouflaged. There were thirty rows of wire entanglements and twelve rows of dragon's teeth. Every inhabited locality was virtually a strongpoint with radio and telephone communications, a hospital, a kitchen and ammunition and fuel dumps. Most of the defence centres consisted of five strongpoints, usually with four pillboxes with machine-guns and artillery. Pillboxes built in 1938–39 had from one to two artillery and three to four machine-gun embrasures and were manned by garrisons ranging from a platoon to a company in strength who lived in underground quarters. Only the top of the structure with the artillery and machine-gun embrasures and an all-round view of the surrounding territory was above the surface. Below were casements, dumps, a kitchen, latrine, corridors, a mess, an officers' room, a machine room, access holes leading to the cupola and an emergency exit. These pillboxes had a reinforced concrete protective covering up to two metres thick. I ordered our gunners to fire at one of the intact pillboxes from close range. The structure withstood a direct hit from a 203mm shell.

In the difficult years of 1939–40, when the Second World War was already on, we substantially augmented our defensive capacity and moved our Western frontiers further to the west almost along their entire length.

SOURCES:

Part I

The Second World War by G. Deborin.

They Sealed Their Own Doom by P. Zhilin.

Part II

Serving the People by K. Meretskov. Translated by D. Fidlon. Published by Progress Publishers, Moscow.

C

The Warsaw Uprising

SUMMARY OF THE WESTERN POSITION

The Poles were the first victims of the Second World War. Fifteen days after Germany invaded Poland's western frontiers, the Soviet army crossed the eastern border. They met with very little resistance not only because the bulk of the Polish Army was engaging the German army, but also because the area eventually occupied (or liberated, depending on your point of view) was largely inhabited by Ukrainians and Byelorussians. Poles at that time were in fact a minority of the population of Eastern Poland. Nevertheless, in the wake of the Red Army advance 300,000 Polish soldiers were made prisoners of war, tens of thousands of civilians were deported and, later, over 12,000 Polish officers, leading statesmen and intellectuals were murdered in the Katyn forest on orders of the Soviet Government.

Some of the leading politicians had managed to escape both the Russians and Germans and make their way to London where they came together to form a broad-based Government. This Government looked after Polish affairs and co-ordinated policy with the Allies while their country was under foreign occupation. Every Polish patriot considered that this Government truly represented their interests. An underground military organization, taking its orders from the leadership in London, was immediately set up inside Poland. This was called the Home Army (Armija Krajowa).

On 22 June, 1941, the invasion of Soviet Russia gave the Poles and the Russians a common cause: the defeat of Germany.

In the second half of 1943 the German army in Russia suffered an almost continuous series of defeats. In 1944 the Red Army crossed the border with Poland and began to liberate Polish territory from German occupation. By this time the Home Army had grown enormously and its thousands of members were well armed, had established good communications with each other and with London, and were organized within an efficient command structure. All this had been achieved in conditions of extreme secrecy and under ever-present threat of death and torture.

As the German troops withdrew, the Soviet Government

created a civil administration consisting of Polish Communists to govern the newly liberated areas. This was called the National Liberation Committee which set itself up as a serious rival to the existing Polish Government in exile in London. The Home Army, while welcoming Red Army help in freeing Poland from German occupation, was determined not to allow a Russian-sponsored Government to be forced on Poland after the war.

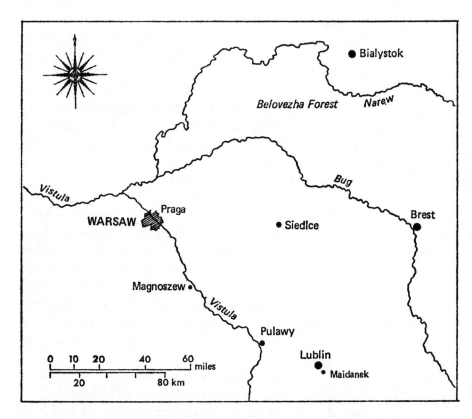

On 30 July the Red Army reached Praga, a suburb of Warsaw, about twelve miles from the centre of the city and on the east of the Vistula. Red Army radio stations called on all Polish patriots to rise up and free themselves from the Nazi invaders. In response to these broadcasts, the whole Army, followed by every underground (including Communist) resistance group fiercely attacked German occupation troops and quickly captured key points in the city. Large areas of Warsaw came under Home Army control. Although the Warsaw Poles had only four days' supply of ammunition, they reasoned that within that time the Red Army

would have entered the city and together they would be able to repel any German counter-attack.

However, for twenty-eight days the Red Army made no move to help the insurgents. The Germans were therefore able to assemble a number of divisions well equipped with tanks, heavy artillery and flame throwers and surround and assault the Polish position.

Desperate pleas for help from any quarter were made by the leaders of the uprising. Churchill sent Stalin a number of telegrams telling him of the severity of the fighting in Warsaw and asking for any help they could give. On 14 August he telegraphed to Eden:

> It will cause the Russians much annoyance if the suggestion that the Polish patriots in Warsaw were deserted gets afoot, but they can easily prevent it by operations well within their power. It certainly is very curious that at the moment when the Underground Army has revolted the Russian armies should have halted their offensive against Warsaw and withdrawn some distance.
>
> For them to send in all quantities of machine-guns and ammunition required by the Poles for their heroic fight would involve only a flight of 100 miles.

The Russians neither advanced their Army, dropped supplies nor gave fighter protection to counter the constant bombing of the Polish positions by the Luftwaffe.

The nearest airfields in Western hands were in southern Italy. To drop supplies meant a flight of 1,000 miles over enemy-held territory without fighter protection. Nevertheless between 13 and 16 August, seventy-nine aircraft flew on supply missions to Warsaw and only twenty were able to make their drops. Thereafter the position became worse, as German anti-aircraft measures increased on the supply route. The Russians even refused to provide for refuelling and repairs on their airfields to British and American aeroplanes. This would have enormously increased the survival ratio of the aircraft and crews on these flights.

Warsaw was destroyed: 250,000 Polish soldiers and civilians killed and the Home Army ceased to exist. One can only assume Stalin had a political motive for wanting their destruction. The leaders of the Home Army would have formed the nucleus of the leadership of a free and democratic Poland after the war. With them out of the way, the Soviet inspired National Liberation Committee could take over the government of Poland without an organized rival.

The Germans had done Stalin's dirty work for him.

THE SOVIET VIEW

On entering Poland we were at once faced with a multitude of complex problems. In the liberated territory, which by now extended to the Vistula, there were many armed Polish groups who had fought the occupying forces: the Gvardia Ludowa, Armija Ludowa, Armija Krajowa, Bataljone Chlopske. There were also mixed guerrilla groups led by Soviet officers who had been stranded or landed on enemy-held territory. The different groups embraced people of every conceivable political affinity drawn together in the struggle against the common enemy.

Now, with the coming of our troops, they received the opportunity of merging into a powerful force.

The Polish civilian population gave the Red Army a very warm welcome. They were obviously glad to see us and did all they could to help rout the Nazi invaders as speedily as possible. As it advanced, the Polish 1st Army swelled rapidly with volunteers from among the local population. Units of the Gvardia Ludowa, Armija Ludowa and other resistance forces joined it. Only the AK—the Armija Krajowa—kept aloof. Our first meeting with representatives of this organization left an unpleasant impression. On receiving information that a Polish formation calling itself the 7th AK Division had occupied the forests north of Lublin, we decided to send out several staff liaison officers to contact them. At the meeting the AK officers, wearing Polish uniform, held aloof and rejected our proposals for combined operations against the Nazis, declaring that the AK took its orders only from the London Polish Government and its emissaries. They defined their attitude towards us in the words, 'We shall not use arms against the Red Army, but we do not wish to have any contacts'. A sticky situation, to say the least.

Meanwhile the Polish National Liberation Committee assumed control as the central authority of the People's Government, and with it the responsibility for handling all such ticklish problems.

At the Polish Government's invitation I visited Lublin, where I met most of its members. They were all patriots of their country and at the same time internationalist revolutionaries. They were shouldering a heavy burden, but were optimistic and in high spirits. I attended a parade of units of the Polish 1st Army and a demonstration of the working people of Lublin. From that time on we maintained the closest contact with the Polish Government.

On 2 August, our intelligence agencies received information that an uprising against the Nazi occupation had started in Warsaw. Startled by the news, the Front HQ immediately went hunting for information to assess the scale and nature of the uprising. It was so sudden that we were quite at a loss, and at first we thought that the Germans might have spread the rumour, though we could not understand its purpose. Frankly speaking, the timing of the uprising was just about the worst possible in the circumstances. It was as though its leaders had deliberately chosen a time that would ensure defeat. These were the thoughts that involuntarily came to the mind. At the time, our 48th and 65th Armies were fighting more than a hundred kilometres east and north-east of Warsaw. Our right wing had been weakened by the withdrawal of two armies to GHQ Reserve, though we still had to overcome strong opposition, reach the Narew and gain a foothold on its western bank. The 70th Army had just taken Brest and was engaged in mopping-up operations in that region. The 47th Army was fighting at Siedlce, its front facing north. The 2nd Tank Army was bogged down on the approaches to Praga, the Warsaw suburb on the east bank of the Vistula, and was busy repelling the counter-attacks of the German armour. The Polish 1st Army, 8th Guards and 69th Armies had forced the Vistula at Magnoszew and Pulawy, south of Warsaw, and were seizing and widening bridgeheads on the western bank: this was the main task of our left wing, a task within their capacity which it was their duty to carry out.

Such was the position of our forces when the uprising began.

Certain carping critics in the Western press did at one time charge the First Byelorussian front and, of course, me as its Commander, with deliberately failing to support the Warsaw insurgents, thereby condemning them to death and destruction.

The Byelorussian campaign had been without parallel in scope and depth. On the front's right wing the advance had exceeded 600 kilometres. Fighting all the way, our forces had strained to the utmost to carry out the tasks set by GHQ. Warsaw, however, could have been liberated only in a new major offensive operation—which was launched later on. In August, 1944, many important measures would have had to be taken to capture Warsaw, even if only as a large bridgehead.

The fact of the matter is that those who had instigated the people of Warsaw to rise had had no intention of joining forces with the approaching Soviet and Polish armies. On the contrary, they had feared this. They had been concerned with other things. For them the uprising had been a political move with the objective of assuming power in the Polish capital before the Soviet troops entered it. These had been their orders from the people in London.

In their mighty westward movement, sweeping aside all obstacles placed in their path by the enemy, the troops of our front had more than fulfilled their tasks by gaining footholds to prepare for a new operation. But it required time to launch it.

To be sure, Warsaw was close, we were engaged in heavy fighting on the approaches to Praga. But every step cost a tremendous effort.

With a group of officers I watched the 2nd Tank Army in action from an OP on the top of a tall factory chimney. We could see Warsaw. A pall of smoke hung over the city, houses were burning amid the flashes of bombs and shells. Obviously, heavy fighting was going on in the city.

So far, however, we had had no contact whatsoever with the insurgents, though our intelligence agencies had made every effort to get in touch with them.

The Polish comrades from Lublin did much to untangle the Warsaw events. We soon found out that the uprising had been organized by a group of AK officers and had begun on 1 August, following a signal from the Polish émigré government in London. The uprising was headed by General Bor-Komorowski and his assistant, General Monter, Commander of the Warsaw Military District. The Armija Krajowa had played a leading part, its units were numerically the strongest, best armed and organized.

All patriotically-minded inhabitants of Warsaw, people burning with hatred of the Nazi invaders and eager to throw the oppressors out as quickly as possible, had joined the uprising. With arms in hand the people of Warsaw tried to smash the enemy. That was their only thought.

However, those who had initiated the Warsaw uprising in that exceptionally unfavourable situation ought to have considered before venturing on this move.

From all that I had succeeded in gleaning from the Polish comrades and the information that had reached the Front HQ, the only conclusion that suggested itself was that the leaders of the uprising were doing their best to isolate the insurgents from any contacts whatever with the Red Army. As time passed, however, the people began to realize that they were being betrayed. The situation in Warsaw deteriorated, bickerings broke out among the insurgents, and it was only then that the AK leadership finally decided to appeal to the Soviet Command—via London.

The Chief of the General Staff, A. I. Antonov, established contact between us and the insurgents immediately on receiving the message of request. On the second day after that, 18 September, the BBC broadcast a report from General Bor-Komorowski to the effect that the insurgents' actions were being co-ordinated with Rokossovsky's HQ and Soviet planes were continuously dropping arms, ammunition and food for them.

Getting in touch with the First Byelorussian front's command presented no difficulty at all. Only the desire was needed. But Bor-Komorowski had decided to contact us only after the British attempt to help the insurgents with supplies from the air had failed. One day eighty Flying Fortresses escorted by Mustang fighters appeared over Warsaw. They flew over in groups at an altitude of 4,500 metres, dropping their load. Naturally, from such a height the cargo was scattered over a large area and much of it failed to reach the insurgents. German AA guns shot down two planes. After that the Allies made no further attempts.

In describing all this I have run somewhat ahead. I shall have the opportunity to return to the Warsaw events again. Now I should like to get back to the fighting in which our troops were engaged.

The enemy had detected a weak point in our positions between Praga and Siedlce, and decided to strike at the flank and rear of the troops that had forced the Vistula, south of the Polish capital. He had concentrated several divisions on the eastern bank in the Praga area, specifically, the 4th Panzer, 1st Hermann Goering Panzer, 19th Panzer and 73rd Infantry. On 2 August, the Germans counter-attacked, but were met on the approaches to Praga by units of our 2nd Tank Army coming up from the south. A fierce head-on engagement ensued. The German troops, with the strong Warsaw defence area behind them, were in a better position.

It was a situation in which the Warsaw insurgents could have tried to capture the bridges over the Vistula, and take Praga by attacking the Nazis in the rear. This would have been a great help to our 2nd Tank Army, and who knows how events might have developed. It, however, ran contrary to the plans of the London Polish Government, which had three representatives in Warsaw, as well as to the plans of Generals Bor-Komorowski and Monter. They had performed their evil mission and disappeared, leaving the people they had provoked into this gamble to pay the price.

The Second Byelorussian front on our right was lagging somewhat behind, while the 65th Army, failing to encounter any appreciable enemy resistance, quickly negotiated the Belovezha Forest—on emerging from which it landed in a trap and was attacked from two sides by units of two panzer divisions. They steam-rollered right through the middle of the Army, carving it up into several groups and for a while cutting the commander off from most of the formations.

At the same time, farther to the west the 4th Guards Cavalry Corps had been forced back to the River Bug north-west of Brest and surrounded there.

These setbacks were reversed by timely and skilful action by the army commanders together with the sending of reinforcements to the threatened areas.

The first half of September saw extensive, protracted fighting often going on well into the night. The enemy strove to destroy our bridgeheads on the Vistula and Narew at all costs. As usual he used Panzers in force, wave after wave attacking Chuikov's troops on the Vistula and Batov's on the Narew. But it was all in vain, and his attacks were repulsed. After losing hundreds of tanks and self-propelled guns and tens of thousands of men, the German Command was forced to concede defeat and assume the defensive.

A breakthrough on the Vistula-Narew line would open the road into Germany proper. That is why the German Command continued a steady build-up of forces and means, striking at our bridgeheads and stubbornly defending their positions on the right bank of the Vistula, with occasional counter-attacks. It was a difficult situation. A powerful enemy group was concentrated in front of Warsaw. It comprised the 5th Viking SS Panzer Division, the 3rd Totenkopf SS Panzer Division, the 19th Panzer Division and up to two infantry divisions. We could not allow this threat to continue and when the 70th Army came up, it was decided to try and rout the enemy forces holding the territory before Warsaw and capture Praga, its suburb. The 47th and 70th Armies, units of the Polish 1st Army, the 16th Air Army, and all the reinforcements that could be spared from other sectors of the Front, were committed to this operation.

On 11 September, the fighting began, and by the 14th the troops had routed the enemy and taken Praga. The infantrymen, tank crews, gunners, engineers and airmen fought with great courage along with the gallant men of the Polish 1st Army. We also received great help in the street fighting from the people of Praga, many of whom gave their lives in the common cause.

This was when the uprising in the Polish capital should have started. A joint strike by the Soviet Army from the east and the insurgents from Warsaw, taking the bridges, could have succeeded in liberating and holding Warsaw, though even in the most favourable circumstances that would have been just about all the front's troops could do.

Our forces cleared Praga of the enemy and came out on the eastern bank of the Vistula. All the bridges joining Warsaw with the suburb were gone.

Fighting still continued in the capital.

Hostilities also continued in the Modlin sector, north of Praga. A relative calm had settled over the Narew bridgeheads, but fierce clashes flared up on the western bank of the Vistula. The troops holding the Magnoszew bridgehead were especially hard-pressed. I must say that we succeeded in holding it largely because the defence was led by General Chuikov, Commander of the 8th Guards Army, who remained in the very midst of the inferno all through the fighting. To be sure, the front command did all it could to give timely help with reinforcements and aircraft.

The tragedy of Warsaw kept worrying me, and the realization that it was impossible to launch a major rescue operation was agonizing.

I spoke with Stalin over the telephone, reporting the situation at the front and everything relevant to Warsaw. Stalin asked whether the front was capable of immediately launching an operation with the object of liberating Warsaw. When I replied in the negative he directed us to give all possible help to the insurgents so as to ease their plight. He endorsed all my proposals concerning how we could help them.

I have mentioned that, starting with 13 September, we had begun to supply the insurgents by air with weapons, ammunition, food and medical supplies. This was effected by our Po-2 night bombers, which dropped their loads from low altitudes at points indicated by the insurgents. In the period between 13 September and 1 October, 1944, front aircraft flew 4,821 sorties in aid of the insurgents, 2,535 of them with various supplies. Our aircraft also gave air cover over districts indicated by the insurgents and bombed and strafed German troops in the city.

The front AA artillery also helped the insurgents with cover from enemy air attacks, while our ground artillery suppressed enemy artillery and mortar batteries. We parachuted several officers into the city for liaison and fire adjustment and succeeded in stopping enemy air raids over insurgent positions. Polish comrades who managed to cross over to us spoke with great appreciation of the effectiveness of our air and artillery operations.

Various insurgent organizations gladly welcomed our liaison officers and fire adjusters. But the Polish patriots warned us that the AK refused to have any dealings with us, and their leadership was behaving extremely suspiciously, fanning hostile sentiments against the Soviet Union, the Polish Government in Lublin, and the Polish 1st Army. It seemed strange that Bor-Komorowski had never even tried to establish direct contact with the front HQ, although the General Staff had provided him with the code. It was obvious that the politicians were prepared to do anything except co-operate with us, and shortly this was confirmed.

For the purpose of extending more help to the insurgents, we had decided to ferry a strong force across the Vistula, to Warsaw. Organization of the operation had been undertaken by the Polish 1st Army HQ. The time and place of the landing, the plans for artillery and air support and co-ordination with the insurgents had all been agreed in advance with the leaders of the uprising.

On 16 September, units of the Polish Army embarked to cross the Vistula. They landed at points on the bank supposedly held by insurgent units, which was what the whole plan had been based upon. But then these footholds were found to be in Nazi hands!

The operation developed haltingly. The first assault succeeded in gaining a foothold with great difficulty. More and more forces had to be thrown into action, and casualties began to soar. Yet the insurgent leaders, far from giving any help to the assault forces, did not even try to contact them.

In such circumstances it was impossible to hold on to the western bank, and I decided to call off the operation. We helped the assault party to return, and on 23 September these units of three infantry regiments of the Polish 1st Army rejoined the main forces.

In undertaking their heroic assault, the Polish soldiers had consciously embarked on a mission of self-sacrifice to help their compatriots. They had been betrayed by men who held the interests of the 'powers that be' above those of the country. Soon we learned that, on instructions from Bor-Komorowski and Monter, the AK units had been withdrawn from the riverfront suburbs into the heart of the city. Their place had been taken by Nazi troops. Among those who had suffered had been units of the Armija Ludowa, whom the AK command had not warned of their intention to withdraw from the riverfront.

From that moment the AK leadership began to prepare for capitulation, which is confirmed by fairly extensive archive materials. Our offers to help those desiring to escape from Warsaw to the right bank were left unheeded. After the capitulation only a few dozen insurgents managed to cross to our side of the Vistula.

The Warsaw uprising thus reached its tragic conclusion.

SOURCE:
  A Soldier's Duty by K. Rokossovsky. Translated by V. Talmy. Published by Progress Publishers, Moscow.

INDEX

Sweden, 113, 122
Syria, 13, 112

Tallinn, 73
Taman Peninsula, 62
Tchaikovsky, 39
Teheran Conference, 65–6
Thälmann, Ernst, 73
Tikhvin, 36
Timoshenko, Gen, 38, 120
Tobruk, 17, 45
Tolbukhin, Gen, 68
Tolstoy, Count L. N., 39
Tripolitania, 46
Truman, Harry, 29, 83, 85
Tula, 35, 39
Tunis, 46
Turkey, 28, 54, 76, 112

Ukraine, 37, 62, 68
United States, 1–13, 16, 29, 30, 40–3,
  46, 66, 69, 78, 84–6, 102, 110–14,
  129
Urals, 32

Vasilyevsky, Marshal, 80
Vatutin, Gen, 51, 62, 68
Velikiye-Luki, 62
Versailles Treaty, 1, 3
Viborg, 107, 113, 114, 120, 122, 123
Vichy, 16, 45
Vistula, River, 72, 80, 128, 131, 132,
  135–8
Vitebsk, 70

Volga, River, 48, 50, 51, 54
Voronezh, 59
Voronov, Artillery Commander, 119,
  120
Voroshilov, K. Y., 97, 98, 118, 120
Vyazma, 59

War and Peace, 39
Warsaw, 71, 80, 127–38
Warsaw Uprising, XVII, 127–38
Washington, 42
Watson (U.S. historian), 99
Western Byelorussia, 11, 12, 27, 109,
  127
Western Siberia, 32
Western Ukraine, 11, 12, 27, 72, 109,
  127
Weygand, Gen, 112, 113
White Sea, 110
Wilno, 98
Wolthat, Helmuth, 95

Yakhroma, 36
Yalta (Crimean Conference), 78
Yaroslavich, Prince Vladimir, 123
Yegorov, Sgt M., 82
Yeremenko, Gen, 51
Yugoslavia, 19, 56, 74–7

Zanolyar, 74
Zeelovsky Heights, 82
Zhdanov, A. A., 30, 117, 120
Zhukov, Marshal, 38, 80, 81
Zvenigorod, 39